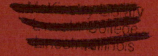

Twayne's English Authors Series

Sylvia E. Bowman, Editor
INDIANA UNIVERSITY

Edward Gibbon

Edward Gibbon

By R. N. PARKINSON

University of Exeter

Twayne Publishers, Inc.   ::   New York

To my family

Preface

Edward Gibbon, the apostle of reasonableness, has much to offer to any age. *The History of the Decline and Fall of the Roman Empire* is the outstanding historical work of the eighteenth century and the greatest work of its kind written in English. The following pages explain how Gibbon's own circumstances and beliefs fitted him to be the mouthpiece of his era in the accomplishment of this immense labor, which was at once a source of delight and of bitter controversy. The delight remains for all succeeding ages: the controversy still continues; and it is the pleasure of any writer on Gibbon to demonstrate how so erudite a historian is at once so amusing and instructive, how the history of the ancient world comes alive under his pen, and how, at the same time, this picture of the past provides a sort of mirror image of the ordered eighteenth-century world which its author so esteemed and admired.

The *History* did not spring spontaneously from an unlabored pen, nor was the detachment of Gibbon's world view arrived at without some experience of intellectual and emotional conflict. The acquisition of his knowledge and the disciplining of his passions were the outcome of a series of painful, hard-won battles with himself and with external circumstance. One of the most attractive features of his writing is the humanity which underlies his most ironical passages.

The *Decline and Fall* is a masterpiece of organization. It sweeps over the whole range of Roman and Byzantine history from the glory of the Empire under the Antonines to the collapse of the last vestige of Roman civilization with the fall of Constantinople in 1453. It is full of battles, sieges, marches and countermarches, together with biographies of the most important historical figures in the Eastern and Western worlds. It contains amusing asides upon the conduct of the ancients as judged by the standards of the eighteenth century; and it is everywhere animated by the historian's satirical asides upon man's unreasonableness. The outstanding feature of the work is its grave and temperate irony which Gibbon claimed to have learned from Blaise Pascal; but the *History* only reveals its full delight to those who can enjoy a demonstration of the perpetual discrepancy between man's ideals and his conduct, without rejecting the claims of idealism or ceasing to struggle for self-improvement.

Gibbon is, in his moderate way, a perfectionist. He is reasonably content with the world as he knows it, but he does not despair of its improvement. At the end of his life, he wrote with satisfaction and gratitude of his own good fortune: "When I contemplate the common lot of mortality, I must acknowledge that I have drawn a high prize in the lottery of life."

Gibbon's style has often been praised, but few critics have appreciated the way in which the actual construction of the *History* reflects his feelings and opinions. My long chapter on *The Decline and Fall* attempts to show how each of the first three quarto volumes was conceived by its author as an artistic whole, which was yet designed to fit into the great master plan. Since the design of the first half of the *History* is clear in the arrangement of the first three volumes, they are treated in detail. The construction of the second half of Gibbon's work is much less sure, and it is, therefore, treated more briefly.

In a later chapter the effects of the famous style (which has been variously likened to minuet time and to the sound of kettledrums and trumpets) are shown to contribute to the maintenance of the philosophical and humanitarian viewpoint. The chapter upon the mechanics of style seeks to exemplify G. M. Young's assertion that Gibbon worked from the theme to the chapter, right down to the point where we can see that each epithet in every sentence counts—that the plan extends to the smallest detail.

Since this study is primarily concerned with the literary merits of Gibbon's work, I have made no attempt to measure *The Decline and Fall* against the results of modern historical research, but I have included in the bibliography a number of books about Byzantine history; and the enquirer should be aware that one writer who praises Gibbon's acumen and grandeur concludes that, "as history, his work is almost obsolete, except for antiquarian details." (Lynn White Jr. in *The Transformation of the Roman World*.)

Acknowledgment of my own indebtedness to many Gibbon scholars is made in the notes and bibliograpy, but I should like here to record my particular gratitude to the *Gibbon* of Mr. G. M. Young which moved me to the study of the historian's life, and to the works of Miss J. E. Norton which have been constant friends and companions during the whole progress of writing. To my colleague Miss K. M. Dexter I am most grateful for a constant and meticulous care in the reading and correction of my typescripts, and to my wife for advice and support at all stages of the work.

R. N. PARKINSON

University of Exeter, England.

Acknowledgments

I am most grateful to the following publishers for permission to make quotations from the works of which they hold the copyright:

Messrs. Ernest Benn Ltd. for a quotation from *Thomas Burt M.P.*; Messrs. Cassell and Company for lengthy quotations from *The Letters of Edward Gibbon*, edited by Miss J. E. Norton; Messrs. Chatto and Windus for lines from *Gibbon's Journal to January 28th, 1763*; and The Hamlyn Publishing Group Limited for the lines from *My Early Life* by Winston S. Churchill.

Contents

Chronology

1737 Edward Gibbon born April 27 (O.S.), May 8 (N.S.).
1747 Death of his mother.
1748 January. Enters Westminster School in the care of his Aunt Kitty (Catherine Porten).
1752 Enters Magdalen College, Oxford.
1753 Converted to Roman Catholicism. Sent to Lausanne, where he stays for the next five years.
1755 Reconverted to Protestantism. His father remarries.
1757 Meets Suzanne Curchod.
1758 May 4, returns to England; spends summer at Buriton; breaks engagement with Suzanne Curchod.
1759 Commissioned a captain in the militia.
1760 Called onto active service with the militia.
1761 Continues service. Stands as M.P. for Petersfield but withdraws before election. Publishes *Essai sur la Littérature*.
1762 December. Militia disbanded.
1763–
1765 His Grand Tour to Paris, Lausanne, Rome, Venice; home by June, 1765.
1767 Begins a history of Switzerland but gives it up.
1768 Vol. I, *Mémoires Littéraires de la Grande Bretagne*.
1769 Vol. II, *Mémoires Littéraires de la Grande Bretagne*.
1770 *Observations on the AEneid*. November 12, his father dies.
1771 Writes *Essay on the Cyropaedia*; never published.
1772 Lets Buriton; Mrs. Gibbon settles in Bath.
1773 Moves into 7 Bentinck Street. First reference in letters to *Decline and Fall*.
1774 Elected M.P. for Liskeard.
1775 Presented at Court. Printing of Vol. I of *Decline and Fall* begins in July.

1776   February 17, Vol. I published. The Neckers in London.

1777   Visits Paris, May–November.

1779   January 14, *Vindication of 15th & 16th Chapters* published. July 2, appointed a Lord of Trade. October, *Mémoire Justificatif* published.

1780   Gordon riots. Loses Parliamentary seat at dissolution. J. B. Holroyd created Baron Sheffield.

1781   June, Vols. II and III of *Decline and Fall* published. Elected M.P. for Lymington. Rents house at Brighton.

1782   Abolition of Board of Trade means loss of £750 a year. Rents house at Hampton for summer.

1783   Decides to retire to Lausanne in a joint household with his Swiss friend Jacques Georges Deyverdun. Takes most of Vol. IV with him in September.

1784   Moves into La Grotte with Deyverdun. Recommences work on *Decline and Fall.*

1786   April 23, death of Catherine Porten.

1787   Visits Britain to prepare last three volumes of the *History* for the press; August, goes to London; visit of Wilhelm de Sévery.

1788   May 8, celebration dinner for publication of last three volumes of *Decline and Fall*; July 30, arrives in Lausanne.

1789   July, death of Deyverdun at Aix; fall of the Bastille in Paris; Gibbon attacked by gout for five months.

1790   Writes part of *Historical Excursions* and essay on *The Position of the Meridional Line.* Starts Memoirs.

1791   The Sheffields visit Lausanne.

1793   Death of Lady Sheffield takes Gibbon back to England.

1794   January 16, death of Gibbon.

CHAPTER I

Life and Times

I   *Early Youth*

F EW writers can have expressed the spirit of their times better than did the English historian Edward Gibbon. In *The History of the Decline and Fall of the Roman Empire*, Gibbon reflects upon the downfall of a civilization which appeared to him, at its best, very much like his own; and the standards by which he judges the great figures of a remote past are the same standards which guide him as an educated eighteenth-century gentleman. He prizes a calm equability of temper, a bland rationality, and a well-informed politeness—qualities which are socially useful and which promote social cohesion. For, like many of his contemporaries, Gibbon remained conscious of the disruptive effects upon the social fabric of the Civil Wars between King and Parliament in the previous century; apprehensive of the dangers inherent in private judgment; and aware of the ludicrous results attendant upon the claim to personal inspiration. Nor did he therefore trust in the good sense of a mere democratic majority: one of the few mentions of the word "democracy" in the *History* is contained in a reference to the "wild democracy of the passions." Gibbon had every reason to fear the guidance of the passions, both in private and in public life.

It has been said, with reason, of the supposed phlegm and *sang-froid* of the English that these attributes do not demonstrate that the English cannot feel; rather, they demonstrate that the Englishman is afraid to feel since he is conscious that his passions, when aroused, may be so violent as to be uncontrollable. This diagnosis was undoubtedly true of the political, religious, and personal passions of Englishmen, individually and collectively, in the great national quarrels of the seventeenth century. One of the greatest philosophers of the period, Thomas Hobbes, who himself witnessed the excesses of his fellow countrymen, found any other miseries "scarce sensible in respect of the miseries and horrible calamities that accompany a Civil War." Even a hundred years

1

and more after these wars, Englishmen feared the effect of private enthusiasm upon public policy. The eighteenth century shows constant evidences of the struggle to maintain public order by a perpetual attention to decency and decorum in private life. The right to express private doubts, to air private difficulties, and to give vent to the deepest emotions is often suppressed by an almost unconscious personal censorship in the interests of security and solidarity. Such suppression may not have been good; eighteenth-century qualities may not have been so excellent or so indispensable as Matthew Arnold thought them; but there is no doubt that large numbers of eighteenth-century men believed, like John Dryden, that common quiet was mankind's concern.

The majority of men who achieved the appearance of tranquility did not do so without a struggle, for passion exists even in the poetry of the man known to the nineteenth century as "cold-hearted Pope." Samuel Johnson, the literary dictator of the mid-century, may have appeared to be a High Church Tory bigot; but the bigotry and dogmatism are intended to reassure himself and his readers. Poets like Christopher Smart and William Cowper never did find in the reasonable arguments and habits of their century the emotional security which they needed, and they in consequence perched perilously over the confines of insanity. The self-control of many an eighteenth-century writer is more evident in his public writings than in his private life.

Gibbon was one for whom the struggle between reason and feeling, between the wish for public approval and the desire for private righteousness, was real and intense; but his conflict was also comparatively brief. The Olympian detachment of style in the *Decline and Fall* was attained long after the intellectual ardors, the religious enthusiasm, and the amorous warmth of youth had been cooled and tempered by the cold waters of rationality and worldly experience. Nevertheless, the memory of those youthful excesses leaves its mark on the whole *History*; and a knowledge of Gibbon's life helps us to understand how he came to achieve and to develop his particular, individual, and yet typically eighteenth-century manner and outlook. In the *History*, we admire the sheer mass of learning, the immensely capacious and retentive memory, the incisive analytical powers, the eye for detail, and the ability to marshal and conduct the intricate marches and counter-marches of a great demonstrative argument. The ground upon which all these qualities rest so firmly is the strongly held emotional conviction that all things are susceptible of explanation by means of a cool rationality. This emotional conviction we may derive equally from

Gibbon's consciousness of the recent history of the English nation and from the personal experiences of his early youth and adolescence.

Gibbon liked to trace his ancestry, with what he himself called a harmless vanity, back to noble forbears. In fact, he was the grandson of a successful London merchant whose family came from Kent. His grandfather, the first Edward Gibbon, had made a substantial fortune, had lost it as a director of the ill-fated South Sea Company, and in the last fifteen years of his life had made another one to leave to his own son. The second Edward (the historian's father) had as his tutor the religious writer and near-saint, William Law; but his tutor's example did not prevent the pupil from indulging in worldly pleasures, once he was free of that firm but gentle guardianship. He made the then-fashionable Continental tour and, as his son was to record later, "resided some time in Paris to acquire the fashionable exercises; and as his temper was warm and social, he indulged in those pleasures for which the strictness of his former education had given him a keener relish."[1] Upon his return to England, the second Edward was chosen Member of Parliament for Petersfield, a borough in which his father had considerable influence; and he also joined the family business. He married Judith Porten, the daughter of another London merchant; and the match was evidently one of genuine affection.

The third Edward Gibbon was born on April 27, 1737 (Old Style). Since, on the evidence of certain passages in the *History*, he has so often been represented as a cold-hearted man, it is worth recording what he remembered of his own childhood. In the *Autobiography*, from which I have already quoted, there is a passage in which he recalls a brief period of "familiar and tender friendship" with his only sister who died in early childhood; and there is no reason to doubt that he did deeply and sincerely regret her death since he remembered it so well some forty or more years later (*Autobiography*, 19). Her place, and the places which five brothers (who all died in infancy) might have taken in his affections, were, in fact, occupied by his aunt and foster mother, Catherine Porten. She died when he was middle-aged and famous; but, when he heard of her death, he wrote to his friend Lord Sheffield that philosophical reflections about death could not dispel a thousand sad and tender remembrances that then rushed upon his mind because "To her care I am indebted in earliest infancy for the preservation of my life, and health. I was a puny child, neglected by my Mother, starved by my nurse . . . without her maternal vigilance, I should either have been in my grave, or imperfectly lived a crooked ricketty monster a burthen to myself and others."[2] After the death of his mother in 1747, his aunt entirely took her place; and, to a great extent, she replaced both parents since his father was fully absorbed by grief and regret for his wife's death and indulged his sorrow in solitude at his manor house of Buriton near Petersfield in Hampshire.

Gibbon attended a day school at Putney for a short period, had a private tutor for some eighteen months, and later attended a boarding school at Kingston "in a lucid interval of comparative health"; but not until he went to live with his aunt did he really begin to develop as a person, for she could give him the constant affection and companionship that his nature needed: "Her indulgent tenderness, the frankness of her temper, and my innate rising curiosity, soon removed all distance between us; like friends of an equal age, we freely conversed on every topic, familiar or abstruse; and it was her delight and reward to observe the first shoots of my young ideas" (*Autobiography*, 26). If the language in which Gibbon expresses his affection is not our own, the warmth of the feeling which it conveys is infectious. This attachment endured for a lifetime, and Gibbon ascribes to her *kind* lessons that early and invincible love of reading which fitted him for one of the principal fatigues of historical research.

In order to earn a living for herself which would enable her to care for her nephew, Catherine Porten kept a boardinghouse for boys at Westminster School, and for two years she watched over his many illnesses while he was a scholar there. During this time, he acquired the thorough grounding in Latin and Greek so common to public schoolboys of his period and so necessary to the success of his future labors. Two years followed of such frequent illness that he was taken from London to Bath, from Bath to Winchester, and from Winchester to Bath again in search of health from the Bath waters and from the advice of celebrated doctors. Removals to Buriton and Putney and another attempt to return to school failed to cure him.

In the course of some desultory journeyings with his father at this time, one incident occurred which marked the bent of his future life. In the summer of 1751 they visited the Hoare family at Stourhead in Wiltshire, and there in the library the young Edward found the *Continuation of Echard's Roman History*. He began to read it one morning, and the work so fascinated him that "I was immersed in the passage of the Goths over the Danube when the summons of the dinner-bell reluctantly dragged me from my intellectual feast" (*Autobiography*, 32). At the age of fourteen, Roman history had for Edward Gibbon the fascination of a detective story and the attractions of a novel.

Six months or so after this episode, his health had so much improved that it was possible for his father to remove him from the care of an unsatisfactory tutor and send him to the University of Oxford. He was sent to Magdalen College, largely because his father did not know what to do with him next; and he entered the college at what, even then, was a rather early age, for he was admitted on April 3, 1752, two weeks before his fifteenth birthday. Gibbon claimed that his early education had been so irregular and so unusual that he arrived at Oxford with a stock of erudition that might have puzzled a doctor and with a degree of ignorance of which a schoolboy would have been ashamed. There he was able to indulge his unusual taste for ancient history and Oriental studies, but he was also allowed by his tutors to waste his time in frequent and lengthy expeditions for pleasure to Bath, London, and Buckinghamshire when he should have been pursuing a plan of organized study.

If Gibbon's work had been adequately supervised, or if he had had the meticulously planned courses which distinguish a modern American college education, he would not have had time to spare for the reading of the religious writers whose persuasions turned him from the Anglican to the Roman Catholic Church. His sudden conversion to Catholicism affected Gibbon's feelings and attitudes for the rest of his life and had a marked effect upon the tone and tendency of his *History*. Several circumstances had prepared him for the change: he had been fond of religious disputation even as a child talking to his aunt; his college, which had a duty to ensure that he subscribed to the Thirty-nine Articles of the Church of England because this was the religious test for entrance to the university, had neglected to require this conformity from him or to prepare him for it—possibly because he was so young; he had been encouraged, by reading Dr. Conyers Middleton's *Free Inquiry* into the nature of miracles, to study the early history of the Roman church; and he was introduced to the Roman Catholic apologists by another young convert at his college. This sequence of events produced the "momentary glow of enthusiasm" which brought about his conversion and raised him above all temporal considerations. There is a marked intellectual pride in his recollection that the reading of Jacques-Bénigne Bossuet finally convinced his reason of the truth of the Catholic doctrine. "I fell by a noble hand," he records with a rhetorical flourish.

In a phrase cited above, Gibbon used a most significant word to describe his feelings at this time. "Enthusiasm" was a term of reproach more than of praise in the eighteenth century, for its associations were all with the religious excesses of the previous century. When in later life Gibbon admitted to having felt this momentary glow of "enthusiasm," he was recognizing a lack of self-restraint and a passionate eagerness to be right, which he now felt to be destructive in tendency. He was admitting the affinity of his emotions as a young man with those of Hudibras—that "errant saint . . . whose chief devotion lies/ In odd perverse antipathies"; and he was ranking himself with those Puritan opponents of Charles II whom Dryden stigmatized as "A numerous host of dreaming Saints . . ./ Of the true old Enthusiastic Breed." The folly of religious enthusiasm was the target of many rational writers well into the eighteenth century, for such self-indulgent emotion accorded ill with the practice of a moderate gentlemanliness. The letter which Gibbon wrote to his father to announce his conversion has not survived, but he recalled it as having been written with all the pomp, the dignity, and the self-satisfaction of a martyr. The convert may have been apprehensive of the results of his conversion, but he was undoubtedly a little self-satisfied with having made an honest sacrifice of interest to conscience.

It would be fairer to regard the self-satisfaction as disinterested than to call it smug, for the conversion could have entailed legal penalties. It was doubtless these results that Gibbon had in mind when he wrote of martyrdom, for conversion to the Roman church was then still technically classified as treason. His father was shocked or frightened or surprised into taking action which, to his son, must have seemed as drastic as anything that an affrighted government might have done. Edward was removed from Oxford and sent to spend a few days with David Mallet, one of his father's London friends, whose skeptic or agnostic views shocked the young convert. Then, on the advice of the Gibbons' wealthy relatives, the Eliots, he was sent to a prolonged banishment in Lausanne under the care of a good Protestant tutor. Under the roof of Monsieur Pavillard, Gibbon was to tread the path back from superstition—at least to skepticism, and probably in fact to the moderate, humanitarian churchmanship of his own century.

The sudden change from the easy and comfortable independence of an Oxford undergraduate with fashionable England as his province to the close and narrow subjection of an alien pupil in an unknown foreign town may have helped to produce the required reconversion, but it was not the main reason for it since Edward soon came to realize the advantages of Pavillard's tuition and to experience his friendship and sympathy. Gibbon's French was not fluent when he arrived in

Switzerland, but he was encouraged to work at it until he spoke it with a native ease. Indeed, it became so natural and habitual to him to think and write in French that he came to have some difficulty in writing idiomatic English in his letters home. On the other hand, some French practices were repugnant: he found his lodgings plain to the point of meanness—he was to remember the "uncleanly avarice" of his landlady; and his very pocket money was under the control of his tutor. From being a man, he was again degraded into the dependence of a schoolboy.

There was undoubtedly some necessity for this control. After he had been in Lausanne for eighteen months, he lost the large sum of one hundred and ten guineas in gambling with a compatriot named Gee, and he was so horrified by his own imprudence that he started for England to raise the money secretly there on the strength of his expectations from his father. There is every evidence in his behavior that cool calculation was no part of his nature in adolescence. The sum he had lost was a very large one for a young man in such modest circumstances. He was only paying about four pounds sterling a month for his board and lodging with the Pavillards, and the prospect of finding a sum equal to more than twice his annual expenditure must have been a daunting one. In an account of the episode to his Aunt Kitty (Catherine Porten), he writes of his despair and of the way in which his thoughts ran upon violent courses of action, recounts that Pavillard's entreaties and persuasions had cut short his flight and brought him back to Lausanne, and begs his aunt to lend him money without telling his father. With sterling good sense, Miss Porten persuaded his father to help and to forgive him, while Pavillard arranged matters in Lausanne to the extent of assisting Gibbon to pay off the remainder of his debts with two guineas a month saved out of his ordinary expenses. Such an experience undoubtedly enabled Edward to see both the folly of gambling and the danger of impulsive action.

Gibbon was deeply indebted to Pavillard for starting him upon the regular courses of study in history, geography, and the French and Latin Classics which laid the foundations of his later reading. His interest led him to relearn Greek and thus prepared him to undertake the researches for his lifework. Among more modern authors whom he read, Blaise Pascal, Jean-Philippe de la Bletterie, and Pietro Giannone remained particularly in his memory. The study of Pascal taught him to manage the weapon of grave and temperate irony; the Abbé de la Bletterie's *Life of Julian* introduced him to this period of Roman history and to the emperor who was to become the outstanding hero of his own *History*; and Giannone's *Civil History of Naples* gave him many of his ideas about the uses and abuses of ecclesiastical power.

Gibbon's conversion to Rome thus produced unexpected and beneficial results, for his five-year exile in Switzerland improved his stock of learning, sharpened his critical faculties, confirmed his bias in favor of ancient history, and began his education as a man of the world. His reconversion to the Protestant religion had equally important consequences in producing that attitude towards the subject of his *History* which gives unity to the whole *Decline and Fall* and in infusing—not without some difficulty—a spirit of greater moderation into his private conduct. To doubt the sincerity either of his Catholicism or of his Protestantism would be to take a false view of his character. He was persuaded successively of the truths of the two faiths by emotion, as well as by the reason of which he speaks himself. If Bossuet had a share in the first conversion, so also had the generous feelings of youth; indeed, he appears to have felt in later life that his first conversion was more of an emotional experience than the second. As long as he felt himself in honor committed to the Roman Church, he was a very loyal Catholic. He was still fasting on Fridays in 1754, and he was a supporter of the grandson of James II, the Roman Catholic Pretender to the English throne. There is a romantic warmth about Gibbon's early attachments, even where they were intellectually well-founded. As an important part of his instruction Pavillard recommended to the elder Gibbon that his son be encouraged to go into society, where he could see and feel that other estimable and pleasant people could think justly upon serious subjects while holding convictions different from his own. This combination of pleasant society, serious study, and regular but friendly disputation worked slowly and surely towards the hoped-for result. Patiently and step by step, Pavillard worked over the ground of his pupil's convictions, until eighteen months of personal sympathy and rational argument turned Gibbon back to Protestantism. The process left him with the lifelong distrust of emotional extremes and of religious fanaticism which was to become one of the main features of his *History*. He had felt within himself the forces which had produced the public violence of the previous century, had observed their effects upon his private life, and ever afterwards distrusted and sought to control them. Having experienced within himself the emotions of religious strife, he finally found it possible and reasonable to give silent consent "to the tenets and mysteries which are adopted by the general consent of Catholics and Protestants" (*Autobiography*, 63). After his struggles, it was no longer necessary for him to argue about his own convictions, because Anglican Christianity seemed to him to represent the most reasonable interpretation of Christian doctrines and to present the most convenient practice of them.

One of the experiences which gave Gibbon more sympathy for the reformed church was a visit made with Pavillard in the autumn of 1755 to the Abbey of Einsiedeln. His tutor thought that the sight of such ecclesiastical splendor in the midst of poverty had done much to confirm his pupil's reconversion. Many years afterwards Gibbon wrote a vivid account of the visit which showed how lively and long-lasting the impression had been, and his description concluded with the reflection "the lively naked image of superstition suggested to me, as in the same place it had done to Zuinglius, the most pressing argument for the reformation of the Church" (*Autobiography*, 78). We may, then, believe that from Christmas Day of 1754, when he received in Lausanne the sacrament according to the Protestant rite, he neither was troubled by religious doubt, nor saw any reason for being so. As a result, the *Decline and Fall* was written by a Protestant who was also a humanitarian in belief and a rationalist in method.

During the remainder of his time in Switzerland, his letters show two distinct and almost entirely separate preoccupations—those of the lover and those of the scholar. His Latin letters to European academics are of great interest because they prove the truth of the claim—which he was to make in his *Autobiography*—that while he was in Lausanne he had read widely and thoroughly in Classical authors and understood them well. According to a modern scholar, his Latin was fluent but faulty; but there is no doubt that he had a command and understanding of the language that most modern Latinists would envy, nor that the acuteness and learning of these letters reveal an early promise of genius hard to parallel.[3] He assured his father of the progress he was making in his studies of French, the Classics, philosophy, drawing, and even dancing (*Letters*, I, 12—13). But study and recreation were not enough to satisfy the need for love and friendship.

While Gibbon was writing learned letters to European scholars, he was also making repeated requests to his father for some sign of paternal forgiveness and affection, but such sentiments seem to have been rarely accorded. He was dismayed in January, 1756, by a change in the mode of address at the beginning of his father's letters from

"Dear Edward" to "Sir"—as an affectionate son might well have been even in days of greater formality than ours—and he assured his father of the depth and sincerity of his own feelings, whilst hoping for some sign of reciprocation. The letters also show that Gibbon's program of reading in 1756 included Suetonius, Quintus Curtius, Justin, and Florus; that he needed a larger allowance and a valet or personal servant; and that he hoped that his father would allow the extra expense incurred by a short trip to Geneva in the summer of 1757; but all his emotions were poured into such impassioned requests as the lengthy, reasoned plea of June, 1757, that he might be allowed to return to England after four years of exile to see his father, his father's new wife, and his much-loved aunt. The formal tone of the correspondence between father and son, the depth of the son's feelings, and the earnestness of his wish to return home may be gathered from another letter written in October, 1757. He writes in French (as he always does) what may be translated thus: "This father formerly so full of kindness has condescended to assure me that all is forgotten and that he will again extend to me his former love. . . ."[4] But he goes on to say: "However, on the other hand, a thousand worrying thoughts crowd in upon my mind. I have written to him many times, I have asked him for indulgences which seemed reasonable and that I hoped to obtain. Nevertheless he remained silent. So cruel a silence torments me, frightens me and makes me imagine the greatest of evils, the loss of his love. . . ."

This language is not altogether the one of affectation, and Gibbon had a new reason for his fears; in his absence, his father had remarried. What would happen to the only survivor of the first marriage, laboring under the effects of his father's displeasure? He hardly dared to ask the question, and he turned, therefore, to his devoted aunt for sympathy and advice. To Miss Porten he wrote in English and in a more natural tone. Evidently she had excused her delays in writing to her nephew on the grounds that he would find her letters dull, for Gibbon's reassurances show the warmth of his feelings and the strength of his need to know that he was loved in return: ". . . not to flatter you, your excuse is a very bad one. *You cannot entertain me by your letters.* I think I ought to know that better than you, and I assure you that one of your *plain sincere letters* entertains me more than the most polished one of Pliny or Cicero. Tis your heart speaks, and I look on your heart as much better in its way, than either of their heads" (*Letters*, I, 35).

A revealing honesty appears in the qualification "better in its way" which is more endearing than all the polished palpitations of his letters in French to his father. When he wrote to his aunt in November, 1756, he told her that he had twice asked his father for an increased allowance and for a servant but without obtaining any reply. So far, he had not dared to ask for permission to return home; but he would do so and hoped to reinforce his pleas by appeals through his other aunt, Hester Gibbon, and his stepmother. As we know, he wrote the dutiful letter to his father which has been cited, but he did not receive permission to return home until the beginning of 1758. By that time, he was involved in quite other feelings and personal relations than those of a dutiful son.

When Gibbon asked his father's retrospective indulgence for the expenses incurred by an unauthorized four-week visit to Geneva, he did not mention any other reasons for the visit than the profit to be derived from travel and from going to the theater; but he was concealing two very important facts: a young Swiss lady called Suzanne Curchod was also staying there, and he had already fallen in love with her. He had first met Mademoiselle Curchod in June, 1757, while he was waiting for a reply to his letters to his father. She was the daughter of a poor Swiss clergyman; but she was attractive, gay, witty, and intelligent. She had been well educated and wrote passable Latin, and she was also very popular with the young people of her circle in Lausanne. Before she and Edward ever met, others had talked to Gibbon of her accomplishments; and, according to the *Autobiography*, "The report of such a prodigy awakened my curiosity; I saw and loved" (*Autobiography*, 83). Undoubtedly the lack of affectionate assurances from his father had disposed Gibbon unconsciously to look for someone who would love him and whom he could love, but Suzanne was not merely a convenient friend; after all his cautions to himself about religious emotion, Gibbon now fell completely and romantically in love for the first time. Even the decorous language of the *Autobiography* makes this fact perfectly explicit: "I understand by this passion the union of desire, friendship, and tenderness, which is inflamed by a single female, which prefers her to the rest of her sex, and which seeks her possession as the supreme or the sole happiness of our being" (82). We may agree with a modern biographer that Gibbon had fallen in love seriously, completely, and honorably.[5] Everything indicates that he was at this time a young man of deep, sincere feelings.

In August, 1757, he was invited to spend two days at Crassy where Mademoiselle Curchod lived with her parents; and, as we know, in

September he went to Geneva for a month to be near her, as well as to improve his mind. His subsequent letters show that he had fallen in love with good sense, intelligence, education, and warm feelings as well as with beauty; and it is easy to believe that all was changed for him after their first meeting (*Letters*, I, 78). He says that he rereads her letters as many as forty-two times, that he loves her entirely, and that he misses her dreadfully—a mixture of simplicity and extravagance that surely shows the sincerity of young love. Since he was sensitive himself, he had to find a means of controling his feelings and protecting himself from ridicule, and such a means was provided by the fashionable kind of allegory which he sometimes uses. It must have been difficult for a young man, without near relatives to whom he could speak simply and sincerely, to use the language of plain love; but the general tone of all the early letters to Suzanne indicates a confidence in her affection for him, together with an increasing tenderness and an awareness of the finer sensibilities.

The young lovers were not given long to enjoy their first happiness. Almost before their first quarrel was well launched, Gibbon was called home. In the very same letter in which he assures Suzanne that there is no foundation for her suspicion that his love is cooling, he tells her that his father has written a most affectionate and friendly letter asking him to return to England. He assures her that his love will make him eloquent in pressing his father to accept their engagement. The most interesting passage in this letter may be translated as follows: "The love of learning was my sole passion up to the time when you made me feel that the heart has its needs as well as the mind and that the heart needs to feel its love returned. I have learnt to love."[6] She had taught him to love. What would become of his love without her continued presence? Would learning resume its disputed empire? Would family affection replace romance? Little by little, exactly this seems to have happened. Gibbon's second excursion into the field of the emotions seems to have suffered the same fate as the first. The passions of the lover passed into the affection of a friend, just as the emotions of the convert had passed into the observances of the orthodox. But neither change was rapid, nor was either achieved without a struggle.

When Gibbon returned to England, he had some idea of the difficulties which awaited him. His last avowals to Suzanne speak of the coming storm; and, sure enough, when the crisis came, his father "would not hear of this strange alliance" (*Autobiography*, 83). In Switzerland, it had been possible to entertain the romantic hope that his persuasions would reconcile his parents to the match; but the nearer he got to England the darker appeared his prospects of success. On April 11, 1758, he started for home, and traveled across France—then at war with Great Britain—dangerously disguised as a Swiss army officer. When the excitement of the journey and the reunion with his aunt and his father were over, he had to make known his new love. He reached London on May 5, 1758, but not until August 24 was he able to write to Suzanne a letter which, in fact, broke their engagement. He explained to her with great care the steps which had led up to this unhappy crisis:

When I arrived in England, both my own feelings and my prospects led me to try to earn my father's love and to disperse the little clouds which had hidden it for some time. I am confident that I succeeded; all his conduct, his delicate consideration for me and his substantial favours made me sure of it. I seized upon the moment when he was assuring me that his dearest wish was to make me happy in order to ask him for permission to offer myself to the lady in whose company all states and all nations would bring equal bliss, and without whom all would bring equal misery. This was his reply. Marry your Foreigner, you are independent, but before doing it remember that you are a son and a Briton. Then he expatiated upon the cruelty of deserting him and of leaving him to an untimely grave and upon the treachery of trampling under foot all that I owed to my country. I retired to my room and stayed there for two hours; I will not try to describe my state to you; I came down to say to my father that I was sacrificing for him the happiness of my life.[7]

While this letter conveys sincere regret, it is evident that the first transports of Gibbon's romantic ardor had been cooled by his return to England, by the welcome he had received, and by his consciousness of what another period of exile might mean to him. We may challenge his fidelity, but we cannot condemn his judgment; for it had really taken three months' residence among his family and compatriots—and not only the two hours of uncomfortable, even painful, meditation in his room—to make him realize that his duty and his inclinations, as well, perhaps, as his self-interest, would be best served by renouncing romance and remaining at home.

What he could not know was that Suzanne's immediate, passionate, hopeful, and reproachful reply had been intercepted by his stepmother, who appears to have warned Suzanne that any other letters would be similarly dealt with. It was not, probably, until February, 1759, that he received what was really her second reply to his letter of renunciation. This second letter, which had been carried to England by a friend and had thus escaped detection, aroused all Gibbon's feelings anew. He demanded the first reply from his parents and then wrote, warmly, passionately, and despairingly, a final lengthy letter of renunciation to the only woman who could have made him happy. Whatever his own wishes, his father would still not hear of this match to a penniless foreigner. Suzanne only replied once more, briefly and brokenly, in a letter which admired but reproached his prudent, dutiful submission; and the affair was over. Gibbon's description in the *Autobiography* of the end of this affair is succinct: "I sighed as a lover, I obeyed as a son; my wound was insensibly healed by time, absence, and the habits of a new life. My cure was accelerated by a faithful report of the tranquillity and cheerfulness of the lady herself, and my love subsided in friendship and esteem" (83–84). The wound was a real one, and it was reopened by Suzanne's reproaches. His cure was not complete until some four years later, when he returned to Lausanne and saw for himself that Suzanne had quite recovered. Thus ended a love affair in which duty to a parent counted for more than passion.

The return from Switzerland marks an important stage of development in Gibbon's life. It began to turn him back into an Englishman, but it did not deprive him of all he had learnt. His studies, his travels, and his friendships had prepared his mind to seek intellectual solace from emotional troubles. He had also acquired standards of behavior and of feeling other than those of the English public-school boy. His religious conversions and his love affair had been instrumental in giving him emotional maturity and in confirming the utility of reason. Many other experiences had contributed to the enlarging of his mind. In Switzerland, he had made the acquaintance of Voltaire and had attended the splendid amateur theatricals at his house; there he had seen for himself the monastery of Einsiedeln, whose magnificence in the midst of poverty had fed his new skepticism about the Roman faith; and there he had made a friendship with a young Swiss, Jacques Georges Deyverdun, which was to have a lasting influence upon his later life. Here was ample material for reflection for a young man of twenty-one.

II *Twenty-one*

Twenty-one was the legal and traditional age of maturity. Gibbon soon found that his father had had other reasons than those of paternal affection for recalling him to England. Now that he was of age, he was able to help his father out of acute financial difficulties by agreeing with him to cut off the entail of the family estate—that is, to free his father from the legal obligation (which had been imposed by *his* father's will) of handing on the family estates intact and unburdened by mortgage to his son. His father was already heavily in debt, and the son's consent to the new arrangement was only a temporary palliative for his difficulties. The inheritance from the first Edward Gibbon had involved complicated legal arrangements: the second Edward had gambled ruinously and had spent carelessly and he had no head for business. Until his father's death in 1770, the third Edward was constantly involved in negotiations to put his father's affairs on a sound business footing and in attempts to persuade his father to consent to them.[8]

Unfortunately, at twenty-one, Gibbon was even less experienced than his father: he could not foresee these difficulties; he was anxious to please; and he consented to the cutting off of the entail in return for an annuity of three hundred pounds, which must have appeared a comfortable sum to live on after his Swiss privations. His father borrowed ten thousand pounds on the security of the legally disencumbered estates and was therefore well content with his son's behavior. Gibbon must have felt the new arrangement to be well worthwhile since it made his newly restored father happy in himself and indulgent to his son.

There had been many things to make Edward apprehensive about his homecoming, and one of the most important was his father's remarriage which Gibbon had construed as an act of displeasure towards himself. He was ready to detest his stepmother as a rival to his mother's memory and as a rival to himself in his father's love. Happily for him, "the imaginary monster was an amiable and deserving woman" (*Autobiography*, 88); and there grew between them a lasting mutual affection which endured the more easily since the second Mrs. Gibbon was to have no children of her own. With genuine concern for his future, she urged him to read law and become a barrister, but she was not offended when he declined the pursuit in favor of a more desultory and dilettante way of life. He was soon able to share with her many of the confidences which he had previously been able to give only to his aunt Porten, and these two ladies were equally loved and esteemed by him to the end of his life.

During the first two years in England, Gibbon lived in London or at

Buriton, the family estate in Hampshire, without any fixed occupation. In London, he was able to enjoy society and the amusements of the town to the limited extent which his own diffidence and his small acquaintance permitted. He was received by Lady Hervey, whose house was a center of French culture; and he was introduced by his father's friend, David Mallet the writer, to a limited circle of polite and literary society. He enjoyed the theater and admired the great actor David Garrick; but he missed the cozy circle which he had enjoyed in Lausanne; he was frequently solitary and continued, perforce as well as by choice, to do a great deal of serious reading.

On his returns to the country, he visited their neighbors with his parents, watched his father farming and shooting, and attended race meetings, though he claimed never to have handled a gun himself and rarely to have sat a horse until he joined the militia. On one occasion he went canvassing on behalf of a parliamentary candidate to the naval towns of Portsmouth and Gosport. This initiation into practical politics, and the disgraceful excitements of eighteenth-century polling undoubtedly influenced his opinion of Roman democracy. His own comment in the *Autobiography* on this particular incident was that the interruption to his studies was "compensated in some degree by the spectacle of English manners, and the acquisition of some practical knowledge" (93).

While at Buriton, Gibbon always rose early in the morning in order to have time to read and study before the long family meals taken together and the visits of friends demanded his whole attention, for he had brought back with him from Lausanne the first fruits of his long course of reading there—the first pages of an essay on literature. All the time he could spare from other claims was devoted to additional reading and to the writing and rewriting of the essay. His father's study contained useful and valuable editions of Classical authors and of the early Fathers of the Church, and Gibbon spent much of his own allowance on the purchase of serious works. His method of study at this time has an interest for readers of the *Decline and Fall* since it helps to explain how Gibbon amassed the information for his immense undertaking. Before he read a new book, he would think over all that he knew about the topic in question so that he could see what new information he was deriving from the work, or what new arguments it gave him to contend with. His studies were methodical, orderly, and accretive; and he read for pleasure the works of such moderns as Joseph Addison and Jonathan Swift, whose style appealed to him as much as their matter. There was some need to study English authors since he still wrote with greater facility in French than in English, and the *Essay on the Study of Literature* which he was polishing and completing was written in the former language.

He had brought fifteen "chapters," or brief sections, of the *Essay* with him from Lausanne and he wrote most of the remaining forty in 1758. The purpose of the work is to show that the Latin and Greek Classics provide the best education for the faculties of the mind. Most interesting is Gibbon's definition of the work of the philosophic historian, as a study of causes and effects which will send us back to first principles. He also warns us—and we may later judge how seriously he heeded his own warning—that religion is difficult to understand when we hate it because our prejudices blind us. The *Essay* was published by Thomas Becket in London, without any prospect of profit for the author, in 1761. Many complimentary copies were sent to friends and to influential persons in England, France, and Switzerland. The work was very well reviewed and most favorably received, and Gibbon could be well content that his labors had procured him some reputation for learning, taste, and intelligence. Best of all, it confirmed him in the pursuit of a literary career, when he turned from practical affairs to renewed studies.

The practical affairs which claimed most of his attention between May, 1760, and December, 1762, were properly the affairs of the nation. England had been at war with France since 1756 and had on several occasions feared invasion from the Continent. In 1759, thirty-six battalions of militia were called up from twenty-three counties to defend the island from invasion, and amongst these was the South Hampshire Regiment. The militia was an army raised on a county basis for home service and chosen by ballot; it was commanded by volunteers from among the local gentry, and both Gibbon and his father had obtained commissions with their local regiment, as a captain and as a major, respectively. They may have joined the militia out of patriotism, but it was also the fashionable and the gentlemanly thing to do. Gibbon confided to his Journal that he had offered to take a commission because his father had done so, without imagining that they would ever actually be called upon for any form of active service, and that, when the call came, it was too late to retreat with honor.[9] As it was, patriotism or harmless vanity had the unexpected result of dragging the father from his farm and the son from his books for two and a half years "condemned ... to a wandering life of military servitude" (*Autobiography*, 104).

Within six months, Gibbon was "sick of so hateful a service" and tired of companions who had "neither the knowledge of scholars nor the manners of gentlemen" (*Journal,* 22). At the end of his time with the militia, his opinion had not changed—they were men of no manners, no conversation, low habits, and despicable character to whom he felt himself in every way superior (*Journal,* 193). But there had been one or two whom he could respect; and, above all, he recognized how valuable a stage of development in his own life had been provided by this taste of military service. Air and exercise gave him unexpected entertainment and improved his health; he gained some practical experience of military life and maneuvers; "and the captain of the Hampshire grenadiers (the reader may smile) has not been useless to the historian of the Roman Empire" (*Autobiography,* 106). He had made many more useful friends and acquaintances than he could possibly have met in a retired life at home. He had learned much about the workings of military organization and about local and central government from his dealings with them as executive officer of his regiment. Most important of all, the daily commerce with his countrymen had turned him back into an Englishman.

For two years and a half, his regiment was marched all over Southern England, but the bustle of camp life did not prevent Gibbon from doing some serious reading. From January, 1761, until the end of his service, he digested lengthy articles from the learned journals of the French Academies, such as Louis Jouard de la Nauze's "Dissertation upon the Ancient Roman Calendar" and Joseph de Guignes's "Mémoire upon the destruction of the Greek Monarchy in Bactriana" (both from the volumes of the Academy of Belles Lettres); and he studied carefully such works as Charles Théophile Guischardt's six volumes of *Mémoires Militaires sur les Grecs et sur les Romains.* This last work, Edward noted, "gives a clear idea of the superior advantages of the Roman entrenchments above our modern ones" (*Journal,* 33, 72); and we see here that his experience of modern methods of warfare had given him a better understanding of the Classical ones. He had also taken up the study of Greek again, and he reread the *Odyssey* and the *Iliad* with great care. Of more modern works he read David Hume's *History of England,* which he found ingenious but superficial, and Voltaire's *Siècle de Louis XIV,* which he enjoyed, although he was critical of the method of the narrative. In fact, he did as much serious reading in his spare time as a soldier as many a modern undergraduate may do in a year or two devoted only to study.

His duties also involved him in visits to the country houses of other gentlemen, and here there are hints of quite different interests. In August, 1761, his heart fluttered for a Miss Chetwynd, whose pleasing person and manner made him wish to see her again. Diffidence, "an idle fear of appearing too particular,"—he means too attentive—prevented him from asking who she was; but the lady appeared again at a ball, and then we hear no more of her (*Journal,* 34—5). In June, 1762, he was introduced to Miss Fanny Page, "a pretty, meek (but I am afraid) insipid girl." Although she had a noble fortune and it had been suggested that he might marry her, she would not do; for "I must have a wife I can speak to" (*Journal,* 83). Mrs. Gibbon even had Miss Fanny to stay with them at Buriton, but Gibbon only discovered that she was no more intelligent than he had thought, and his stepmother's matchmaking was a failure. The third lady who appears in the Journal is a Miss Caryll, whose "French freedom and manly courage make her appear more a man than a woman; nothing boisterous but a very pretty genteel sensible man" (105—106). There is a trace of caution rather than sentiment in these entries—and there is no mention whatsoever of Suzanne. At twenty-five, Gibbon found that the gay vanity of youth no longer fluttered in his bosom; and his affections were firmly set on safer subjects than young ladies.

Among the accounts of his reading which his Journal gives for 1762, we find the almost irrelevant sentence declaring that he cannot sufficiently express the pleasure he feels at meeting his stepmother at Bryanstone, the Portmans' house, because "I love her as a companion, a friend and a mother" (72). He wrote long letters of cheerful gossip to her from his camps and asked her to perform such commissions as sending on his copy of Strabo's *Rerum Geographicum,* when he had carelessly left it behind (*Letters,* I, 127—29). A similar devotion continued to bind him to his aunt Porten whom he visited whenever he could, out of the "friendship, gratitude and confidence which contribute chiefly to attach me to her" (*Journal,* 202). Both these were ladies with whom he could enjoy the exchange of confidences without the need for romantic complications; and, after his renunciation of Suzanne, it was to such relationships that Gibbon turned for the emotional stability which he needed.

Such a confidential relationship he was already hoping for, while still in the militia, with his Swiss friend Deyverdun. An unexpected letter from him ("I had never forgot him but was afraid he had me") made Gibbon recognize him to be "from his character and way of thinking . . . the only friend I ever had who deserved that name" (*Journal,* 82);

and he expressed to his Journal the wish that he could find out any scheme of their living together. Evidently, he did think up some such scheme and was very much taken with the whole idea, for he wrote an eight-page reply to Deyverdun, pouring out his whole soul to his friend (the phrase is his own) and proposing to him projects which are not even entrusted to the pages of the Journal. This wish to enjoy his friend's constant companionship was only granted many years later: in the meantime, Gibbon made the most of his new-found freedom from military duties.

His first wish was to travel, and he obtained permission and funds from his father to go to Paris and Lausanne. He had the intention of traveling farther if allowed to do so; but he seems to have set out with his father's consent to go only one step at a time on what might eventually become a Grand Tour. Such a Continental journey, lasting two or three years, was the normal completion of a wealthy young Englishman's education; and Gibbon had long looked forward to this possibility. While still in the militia, he had urged his father not to go to the useless expense of buying a rotten borough for him since he preferred travel to the glory of a seat in Parliament. A brief experiment had convinced them both of the rightness of Gibbon's choice (he had withdrawn from a parliamentary contest for Petersfield in 1761 without too much loss of money); and in January, 1763, Gibbon left for Paris, alone.

In one respect his way was well prepared by the publication of his *Essai sur l'Etude de la Littérature*, whose modest renown had ensured him a flattering reception in the French capital. He was a little chagrined by his letters of introduction, which made him appear the literary man rather than the gentleman by birth, but he was well received in the capital of manners and taste. He said that he enjoyed best the society of those who dined at home, were glad to see their friends, and passed the evenings until about nine in agreeable and rational conversation (*Letters*, I, 133). By the beginning of February, 1763, he felt completely at home in Paris; and he claimed to have heard more conversation worth remembering and to have seen more men of letters among the people of fashion in two weeks of life in Paris than he had done in two or three winters spent in London.

If he found that English dukes were only coldly civil to him, he had all the excitement of an introduction to the philosopher Helvetius, whom he found to be a man of feeling, intelligence, and wealth; and he enjoyed the good dinners of a large number of hostesses who made a great fuss over him and who enabled him to meet others. He could—and did—dine regularly each week at the houses of Madame Geoffrin, of Madame du Bocage, of Helvetius, and of the Baron d'Holbach, in order to meet d'Alembert, Diderot, and a host of other famous figures. He wrote to his father: "Their men of letters are as affable and communicative as I expected ... My book has been of great service to me, and the compliments I have received upon it would make [me] insufferably vain, if I laid any stress on them" (*Letters*, I, 136).

The charms of Paris were increased by the popularity of the British who had just won the Seven Years' War against the French and were in consequence admired by their late adversaries. Gibbon enjoyed immensely the freedom to live on his own, the money to dress fashionably, the privacy of his own apartment, the dash of his own carriage—an elegant *vis-à-vis*—and the comfort of an excellent Swiss servant who accompanied him on all his travels. For the first time he really felt himself to be something of an independent man of the world and every prospect pleased him.

Life in Paris was too expensive for him to be able to stay there any longer than three months, and he set out in May, 1763, for Lausanne, where he found the society so congenial that he spent the next eleven months there. Letters to his father and stepmother bespeak his satisfaction with the calm, temperate, studious life which he lived there. His reading list was again a formidable one, and this time it was designed to enable him to map out a description of the ancient geography of Italy as a preparation for the projected tour.[10] He intended to go well equipped and perhaps to earn some fame as the author of a learned guidebook to the Grand Tour. At this stage, and even later, while traveling in Italy, he had only thought of producing "something by way of a Description of ancient Italy which may be of some use to the publick and of some credit to myself" (*Letters*, I, 181). His course of study was very much enlivened and interrupted by his renewed adherence to a club of young people, "La société du printemps," in whose company he found constant pleasure and refined amusement. His lodgings with Monsieur de Mésery were very comfortable, and his landlord was hospitable. He had time to revisit Voltaire and to criticize with a more experienced eye the dramatic performances of the aging philosopher and his niece. He was drawn into other affairs, including the prevention of a duel between two of his acquaintances. He had now become a man of the world.

When he left Lausanne, however, it was with less regret than upon the former occasion, for this time he left only acquaintances behind: last time, it had been a dear friend and his beloved. His return to the home of Suzanne Curchod cannot have been without apprehension; in fact, while he was in Lausanne, that lady wrote him three appealing letters which invited him to renew their tender relationship. Her account of her long wait for his return and of her faithfulness to his memory wins our sympathy, but Gibbon had genuinely decided not to marry and his earlier passion faded into friendship and esteem. Indeed, the former lovers parted with something like coldness on Gibbon's side; it may have been that this was the only way to convince Suzanne that her last hopes were in vain. Gibbon's praise of the agreeable calm of Lausanne shows his unfitness for the excitements of matrimony: as he was to write much later," celibacy is exposed to fewer miseries"—though he felt that only marriage could promise real happiness "since domestick enjoyments are the source of every other good" (*Letters*, I, 214). By 1763, if not before, he had consciously, sensibly, and practically chosen to live unmarried as a part of his plan to become a historian (*Autobiography,* 117).

While Gibbon was away, he felt it necessary to seek his father's approval for all his expenditures. More than once his father wrote to him about fresh financial difficulties and Gibbon's acute uneasiness about money certainly influenced his decision not to marry; however he appealed to his father for permission to complete the Grand Tour on the grounds that the journey was really a capital investment in his own intellectual improvement. At last permission was forthcoming, and in April, 1764, he set off for Italy in the company of William Guise, the young Englishman whom he had prevented from fighting a duel in Lausanne. The tour was a lengthy one, and it was a great success. Guise proved to be a most congenial companion, and the two traveled together all over Italy for about twelve months, until Gibbon was called home by his father.

His comments on all that he saw are those of a good Protestant Briton: he was as impressed by the degraded condition of the porters who carried him over the Mont Cenis pass as by the grandeur of the mountains; he was dubious of the value of the ceremonial of the Sardinian court at Turin; and he admired evidences of the free democratic spirit of the Genoese who had obtained their freedom from Austria. He set out conscientiously to obtain the greatest possible cultural benefits from the tour: in Florence, he studied art treasures with all the assiduity of a modern tourist armed with his Baedeker. The details which he gives in his Journal of fourteen visits to the Uffizi Galleries show his intention of making a descriptive catalogue of all the art treasures seen on his journey. The excitement and interest of travel, the daily cares and annoyances, the distractions provided by friends and his own laziness prevented him from doing more than sketching a skeleton plan of impressions which he intended to fill out from memory later on. Rome proved an irresistible attraction, and all the little mortifications of travel which he had felt in dealing with "the vilest part of mankind, Innkeepers, post masters and custom house officers" (*Letters*, I, 181) were amply repaid by the excitement of finding himself there at last.

His reading and researches had prepared him to enjoy the spectacle, but the reality of Rome so far outweighed his expectations that he felt himself to be in a dream: "Whatever ideas books may have given us of that people, Their accounts of the most flourishing state of Rome fall infinitely short of the picture of its ruins. I am convinced that there never [before] existed such a nation and I hope for the happiness of mankind that there never will again" (*Letters*, I, 184). Even twenty-five years later, when he wrote his *Autobiography*, he recalled the strong emotions which had agitated his mind as he approached Rome. So strong were these that he applied the word "enthusiasm" to them and admitted the well-nigh romantic fervor which animated him during most of the eighteen weeks of his stay: "several days of intoxication were lost or enjoyed before I could descend to a cool and minute investigation" (*Autobiography*, 159).

Gibbon made as thorough and minute an inspection of the art and antiquities of Rome as his time would permit; and, if his powers of attention were sometimes fatigued, the first enthusiasm only ripened into an ever-warmer interest and regard. If Gibbon had a real love affair in later life, his mistress was certainly ancient Rome. Nothing can improve upon his own brief account of the momentous result of his visit: "It was at Rome on the 15th October, 1764, as I sat musing among the ruins of the Capitol, while the barefoot friars were singing vespers in the Temple of Jupiter, that the idea of writing the decline and fall of the city first started to my mind" (*Autobiography*, 160).[11] All his serious reading, his studious inclinations, his travels, and now this overwhelming emotional experience pointed out to him on this day in 1764 the one serious and satisfying occupation of his life; and, during the next few years, however much distracted he was—by family affairs and public duties—from the writing of a Roman history, the aim and feeling which had inspired it remained fresh within him.

Nothing impressed him more than the city of Rome, but he also enjoyed his six weeks in Naples and a short visit to Venice. His letters were enlivened with descriptions of his acquaintances as well as of antiquities, for he visited other Englishmen who were traveling abroad, as well as the Italians to whom he had introductions. This pleasant life had, however, been interrupted several times by letters from his father about money difficulties; and, when he reached Lyons on the return journey, he found that his father was urging him to return home in June as he had originally promised. Financial worry, as well as family feeling, prevented him from lingering in France, and he arrived back in London on June 25, 1765, after two and a half years of higher education. Edward managed, however, to pay one important visit on the way. He passed through Paris and stayed there several days because he was treated very civilly by Monsieur Necker, a Swiss banker (who later became Director of Finance to Louis XVI) and by his new wife—no other than Suzanne Curchod. She was not averse to showing him the grandeur of her new position, and he was happy to find these friends in Paris. In an easy, chatty letter to one of the friends whom he had made while he was in Lausanne (this was John Holroyd, to whom any biographer of Gibbon is immeasurably indebted) he gave this comic account of his supposed chagrin at the familiarity of his reception: "Could they insult me more cruelly. Ask me every evening to supper, go to bed and leave me alone with his wife; what an impertinent security. It is making an old lover of mighty little consequence" (*Letters*, I, 201).

This reaction is his English response to French politeness: several times during his travels Gibbon felt that his experience of foreign government and manners was making him a better Englishman. The pride, vice, and slavery which he had seen in the kingdom of Naples were not compensated by more elegant manners or by more refined arts; and he was prepared on his return to England to admire the plain honesty and blunt freedom of his own countrymen. This satisfaction with things as they were in England helps to explain Gibbon's apparent subsidence into contentment with the life of an English gentleman of no fixed occupation.

From 1765 to 1770, the year of his father's death, he was a dutiful and dependent only son. He was able to indulge his own wish to write; he had the company of his close friend, Deyverdun; he could live on his own in London for part of the year and find a refuge in the country at Buriton when he chose to join his family. His relations with his father had enormously improved and his stepmother had become a real friend and confidante. The one perpetual and continuous cause of disquiet was his father's carelessness in money matters. The memoirs and the letters show that it was Gibbon's real affection and respect which prevented him from insisting, as in logic he should have done and as in practice he tried to do, that his father should settle matters with his creditors and secure a sufficient income to his wife and to his son before his death.

Gibbon now began to prepare himself by practice in writing for the composition of his greatest work, and he was encouraged in this by the presence in London of his greatest friend. In one of the drafts of the *Autobiography*, Gibbon ranked Georges Deyverdun with Suzanne Curchod as the dearest friends of his youth and as one of "the two persons who possessed the different affections of my heart."[12] The warmth of his feelings for Deyverdun is betrayed by the language which, after his friend's death, he used to describe this friendship. It is almost worthy of a sentimental novel of the period: "Mr. George Deyverdun ... was a young Gentleman of high honour, and quick feelings, of an elegant taste and a liberal understanding: he became the companion of my studies and pleasures; every idea, every sentiment was poured into each other's bosom: and our schemes of ambition or retirement always terminated in the prospect of our final and inseparable union."[13] Deyverdun had had to earn his living as tutor to the Margrave of Schavedt in Germany. When this task was cut short by an honorable but unrequited love, he came to London to look for similar employment, and Gibbon obtained for him in the first instance a humble position as clerk in the office of the Secretary of State.

In the meantime, he was Gibbon's partner in two literary ventures. The first was a history of Switzerland, the country whose free spirit they both so much admired. Deyverdun's knowledge of German enabled him to translate for his friend the works written in that language which Gibbon needed to know, and during 1765 and 1767 this preparation for the actual writing went forward. The two were "allowed" to spend the summers at Buriton in reading and writing (Gibbon's use of the verb "allowed" implies that his father was suspicious of male as well as female foreigners, or perhaps that he was jealous of anyone who absorbed any of his son's affections); and in the winter the first part of the history of Switzerland was read aloud, anonymously, in its author's presence to a literary society of foreigners in London. He was sufficiently abashed by their comments to suppress the work; but Hume, who was asked for his opinion of the fragment, thought very highly of it. What most influenced Gibbon in his suppression of the work was the fact that he had written—under the influence of Deyverdun and of his old habits—in French, and he thought that this had encouraged him to fall into a "verbose and turgid declamation" (*Autobiography*, 166).

The next joint venture was still designed to appeal to a Continental audience: between them, the two friends wrote and published a review of the literature, arts, and manners of Great Britain for the year 1767, called *Mémoires Littéraires de la Grande Bretagne*. Several such journals, designed to keep foreigners informed of the progress of English literature, had already appeared abroad during the century, but this journal was the only one of its year. While it had something of a *succès d'estime*, it did not sell well; and the authors had to find a new publisher for their second volume which treated the year 1768. This sold even fewer copies and, perhaps fortunately for the self-respect of the two, Gibbon found his friend a new job as tutor to Sir Richard Worsley, which took him abroad before a third volume (which might have fared worse) could be completed. Gibbon could not remember, when he came to write his *Autobiography*, which partner had been responsible for each individual article because constant collaboration had produced a virtual identity of thought, style, and feeling.

When Gibbon was left on his own again, he started at last to write in English; and his first English work was a short pamphlet, published anonymously, *Critical Observations on the Sixth Book of the Æneid*, which attacked cogently, concisely, and convincingly Bishop Warburton's allegorical interpretation of the Sixth Book. It was published in 1770, and Gibbon later regretted that the pamphlet had been anonymous and that it had been so personal. It was commended by critics of the day as "judicious and spirited," "a most clear, elegant and decisive work of criticism."[14] Although Gibbon's tone was unkindly satirical of Warburton, his criticisms were justified; and the pamphlet is evidence of the width of his reading, the acuteness of his critical faculties, and the elegance of his English style.

In this year, 1770, the departure of Deyverdun and the death of his father were events which left Gibbon little leisure or inclination for writing. The years before his father's death had been troubled by attempts to bring order into the family finances, and the two succeeding years were equally perplexed. Both 1771 and 1772 were spent between Buriton and London, making up his mind what to do next. In all his financial affairs he now began to lean heavily on the advice and friendship of his old acquaintance John Baker Holroyd, who later became Lord Sheffield. Although Gibbon knew enough about farming to sell his hops advantageously as "Farmer Gibbon," he agreed with Holroyd that he was wasting his time in the country. The sense of importance which his situation as a landed gentleman gave him did not repay him for the dullness of country life, and even his strong sense of duty did not reconcile him to the necessity of living all the year at Buriton with his stepmother. A woman and a philosopher would not, he felt, be efficient partners in farming.

He chose, therefore, to live in London and to sell his troublesome country estates. Mrs. Gibbon was at last convinced of the foolishness of staying at Buriton for sentimental reasons alone, and she resigned herself to the comforts of Bath and an annuity. Her stepson wrote to her there kindly rather than frequently, but he also visited her dutifully and on one important occasion they took a holiday together. In September, 1773, they stayed with the Eliots, Gibbon's cousins, in Cornwall, where Gibbon had an eye upon the family's political patronage. Delicacy prevented him from proposing himself as candidate for one of the parliamentary seats controlled by his cousin, but the visit produced the desired consequences in the following year.

Mrs. Gibbon followed his doings with minute interest for the rest of his life; and he writes to her with similar equanimity and amusement, whether he is describing his new wallpaper or denying the rumor that he is to marry Miss Holroyd. It is largely from his letters to her and to Holroyd that we can discover with what pleasure he took up his new life of independence and comfort. At the end of 1772, he was settled in a house of his own in Bentinck Street, Cavendish Square, in which he could enjoy solitude or society at his own choice. By the standards of his age, he was modestly comfortable rather than wealthy; and he had some reason to be grateful for this modest affluence since he came to believe that greater wealth or poverty would have prevented him from undertaking his great work. As it was, he had been moving steadily towards the grand object which he had set himself while in the Forum at Rome. Even in the busy years of 1771 and 1772 he had reviewed much of his material: in 1773, he actually sat down to write.

London had many time-wasting attractions, but it also supplied a stimulus to his writing which Buriton could never have given, and the letters show a great liveliness and variety of activity during the whole period of composition of the first volume of his *History*. By September, 1773, the month of his Cornish visit with Mrs. Gibbon, he was well into the work; a year later he had found a publisher ready to print 750 copies; and in June, 1775, the first volume was almost ready for the press. This achievement appears all the more remarkable when we see what a variety of occupations he had besides.

One morning at half past seven, "as I was destroying an army of Barbarians" (*Letters*, II, 32), his cousin Eliot came to offer him the parliamentary seat of Liskeard. Gibbon was delighted to accept this offer since a seat in the House would assure him greater social importance than he could enjoy as a private gentleman and would put him in a better position to supplement his private income by acquiring some lucrative government office. He was therefore willing to pay a large part of the election expenses himself by means of a *post mortem* bequest to his cousin's children. Even at this moment, however, he had secret hopes of earning enough from his *History* to pay the election expenses in the near future, thus making the bequest unnecessary. Within a month, the election was over and won: Gibbon heard of his victory on October 14 without even going to Cornwall; for such were the advantages of a pocket borough.

Throughout the momentous events of the 1770s, which gave independence to America, Gibbon supported the home government against the colonists and suppressed, in public at least, his many misgivings. He never spoke in Parliament, but he showed a historian's awareness of the importance of the colonial rebellion. His letters are dotted with frequent references to the progress of the war, which sometimes seems to preoccupy him to the exclusion of his work. At the end of his first parliamentary session in April, 1775, he hoped that, with firmness, the American war might soon be over. He wrote somewhat ruefully to Holroyd "for myself having supported the British I must destroy the Roman Empire" (*Letters*, II, 69).

A letter to his stepmother shows that the bustle of parliamentary life and even the long sessions were agreeable to him. He wrote, with a hint of self-importance, "I have really had a very considerable hurry of new Parliamentary business: one day for instance of seventeen hours, from ten in the morning till between three and four the next morning. It is upon the whole an agreable improvement in my life and forms just the mixture of business of study and of society which I always imagined I should, and now find I do like" (*Letters*, II, 63). He constantly transmitted the latest news from America in his letters to Holroyd at Sheffield Place; and he came finally to feel that the home government had been dilatory, ineffective, and foolish in its assessments of the situation and in the measures it had taken; but, being equally inculpated himself, he made no grand gesture of resignation. The House of Commons was after all a very gentlemanly club.

III *Splendid Success*

Deyverdun visited England several times with his different pupils, and on one occasion Gibbon took both his friend and his Aunt Porten on one of his visits to his stepmother at Bath. The latter's concern for his well-being resulted in at least one new proposal to marry him: he found her candidate, a Mrs. Ashby, an agreeable woman, though not handsome; but there seems to have been some objection to the lady on the score of her too-great devoutness. He may have taken the proposal quite seriously, although in comic deprecation he signed one of his letters treating of the matter *Benedict* Gibbon (*Letters*, II, 48—9, 63). Though he rejected the lady, he was pleased to accept a domestic pet sent by his stepmother, a Pomeranian bitch to which he gave the name Bath (in celebration of her place of retirement); and he was pleasantly diverted by this "pretty, impertinent, fantastical" lady whom he declared to be the comfort of his life.

A more serious and long drawn-out occupation was his carrying out of the duties of executor to the will of his friend Godfrey Clarke, a process which for some years involved him in negotiations and sometimes provided him with a useful excuse for not leaving town. He was also presented at Court, but this did not seem to interest him so much as his visits to Bath and to Sheffield Place. The letters which tell us of his interests are written in a style very different from that of the *History*, and they show him to have been cheerful, good-natured, and unaffected during the whole period of his writing. He can rejoice that Deyverdun is to have an annuity of one hundred pounds as a reward for tutoring Alexander Hume, or he dashes off to attend his stepmother through the smallpox with equal pleasure or concern. It is easy to forget the historian through interest in the human being.

From June, 1775, however, he had to decline all invitations in order to correct the proof sheets of the first volume of *The Decline and Fall of the Roman Empire* as they came from the press. He had to excuse himself from visiting the Holroyds on the grounds that the work had begun printing before he had quite finished writing it; but, in answer to this friend's warnings about premature or over-hasty publication, he declared that the part being printed had been completed and revised in the two previous years and that the end had been perfectly formed and digested, and had indeed been written down: all he had to do was recast the ecclesiastical part. Privately, he believed his own work to be good, and he hoped that it might be excellent; but he did not trust his own judgment and was both pleased and surprised when his publisher asked him for permission to double the size of the first edition before he had printed more than the first twenty-five sheets of the book.

It was during this process of revision in October, that he rushed to his stepmother's bedside in Bath while she was ill, confiding ruefully to Holroyd that the doctor (who could not pronounce her out of danger) "knows not the value of time, when the fate of an Empire depends upon it" (*Letters*, II, 86). The following January he was still correcting proof sheets and anticipating, with one auspicious and one dropping eye, the probable fate of the work. He had not confessed to his stepmother until June, 1775, that he was engaged in a great historical work; but he betrayed all his hopes and anxieties to her in a letter written early in January, 1776:

The Public I know not why except from the happy choice of the subject, have already conceived expectations, which it will not be easy to satisfy: the more especially as lively ignorance is likely to expect much more, than the nature and extent of historical materials can enable an author to produce. However if the first volume is decently received in the World, I shall be encouraged to proceed; and shall find before me a stock of labour and amusement sufficient to engage my attention for many years. The prosecution of some scheme is in my opinion the most conducive to the happiness of life, and of all schemes the best is surely that the success of which chiefly depends upon ourselves (*Letters*, II, 93-94).

His expectation was amply satisfied and his fears put at rest when the first volume of *The Decline and Fall of the Roman Empire* appeared on February 17, 1776. An instant success, the edition sold out in fifteen days; and, to use Gibbon's words, it was "very well received by men of letters, men of the world and even by fine feathered Ladies" (*Letters*, II, 100). A second edition was immediately called for. Gibbon celebrated his triumph by making a long-promised, duty-visit to his stepmother early in April, although his success had made him eager to start immediately upon the second volume.

The author's satisfaction with the reception of his book can be seen in a long letter which he wrote to Deyverdun early in May. In this letter of frank and unashamed enjoyment, he sets out his earlier fears of public opinion, his gratification at the generous praise of such distinguished historians as Robertson and Hume, his pleasure that politicians of both parties admire the *History*, and his frank delight in the flattery of fine ladies—particularly when they are young and pretty and not too fat. Only one thing galls him: the clergy accuse him of satirizing religion. He is anxious that Deyverdun should immediately begin the translation of the work into French: the first sheets of the book have all been sent direct from the press so that the translation can be made quickly, and the *History* can then be read (and perhaps burnt for its freedom) all over Europe.

The Neckers' visit to London in April gave additional pleasure to his triumph. He and Suzanne were delighted to see one another again. Gibbon thought that she was no longer a beauty and found it all the easier to resume the friendship of their youth, laughing a little at her Paris varnish and encouraging her to be a simple reasonable Swiss instead of a fine lady (*Letters,* II, 103, 109). She admired his work and enjoyed his company so much that he was easily persuaded to promise a return visit to Paris in the coming year. Meanwhile, he was occupied with the corrections to the second edition of Volume I, his steady progress with the writing of Volume II, his regular attendance (by way of recreation) at the anatomy lectures of Dr. Hunter, visits to "that giddy girl," his ever-youthful aunt Porten, and frequent sittings at the distressing sessions of Parliament, which continued to preside over the dissolution of the American colonies. Gibbon had also to face increasing criticism of the last two chapters of Volume I by the learned Dr. Watson of Cambridge and the ill-natured Mr. Chelsum of Oxford and to arrange for the translation of his work into French by Leclerc de Septchènes, since Deyverdun had found himself unable to undertake the task. Always in the background there was the tiresome continuance of the business difficulties inherited from his father.

However, in 1777, he took a six-month vacation from all these employments by paying his promised visit to the Neckers in France. His stay in Paris gave Gibbon the greatest possible pleasure because he was received everywhere with friendship and marks of distinction. The aged Madame du Deffand and the Duke of Choiseul were equally eager to meet him; he dined by accident with Benjamin Franklin; and he had the pleasure of being able to pursue his researches and of persuading the distinguished geographer Jean Baptiste d'Anville to prepare maps for his *History*. He left Paris with regret, but he was soon reabsorbed by his writing when he returned to London in November, although he had an attack of gout upon his return.

The year 1778 was full of worries from which even the constant help of Holroyd could not save him. His tenant at Buriton was unsatisfactory, his bank was calling in money loaned to him, Mrs. Gibbon was in need of a larger income to support life in Bath, and he had to sell some of his assets. In consequence, he toyed once more with his plan of living in Switzerland which would have been much cheaper than England, but he also hoped that his support of the government and his friendship with Attorney General Wedderburn might result in his being offered some lucrative government office. In June, 1779, his hopes were realized: he was made one of the Lords of Trade and assured of a comfortable income. Throughout this troublesome period he was working hard on the next volume of his *History*, an occupation which he felt to be at once the pleasure and the honor of his life. Events in America gave his work an additional relish: he felt that the declines of the two Empires—the Roman and the British—were advancing in parallel steps. Shortly after his new appointment, he wrote his *Mémoire Justificatif Pour Servir de Réponse à l'Exposé de la Cour de France*, an answer to a French attack on British policy, made on behalf of the British government. This work was so well written that the anonymous author of the pamphlet was thought to be a Frenchman, and it obtained the highest praise in foreign courts. In this century it has been recognized as one of the most ably composed and entirely readable state papers ever issued.[15]

He was also finding that the subject of his Roman history had grown so much under his hands that it would fill two new volumes instead of one. The additional pressure of work entailed by this expansion of his material prevented him from going to visit his stepmother in Bath as often as she might have wished, but his increasing occupation brought solid compensations to Mrs. Gibbon. His new post enabled him to increase her income by half, from two hundred to three hundred pounds a year, so that she could live in comfort. But, when Parliament was dissolved in 1780, his cousin declined to give him any more support at Liskeard; and his friend Wedderburn found him the borough of Lymington for which he was elected in June, 1781, without ever going to see his electors. Although he professed to be tired of Parliament, it was only the income of his office which enabled him to continue to live in England and to meet many of his friends on terms of equality.

In June, 1780, he was busy revising and correcting the next two volumes for the press. His real concern for accuracy and comprehensiveness is shown by the fact that, even at this late stage, he was eager to see some of Isaac Newton's papers on Athanasius, of which he had just heard, before he sent to the press that part of his second volume which related to that figure. A most surprising event then upset the summer tranquility of the capital—the Gordon riots, which would be interesting to us if only for the reaction which they provoked from Gibbon. He was seriously alarmed at riots led by "flagitious criminals" because they contradicted all his hopes and expectations for the continued improvement of mankind and cast his mind back to the dark passions of the seventeenth century. He wrote to Mrs. Gibbon at the end of the month: "Our danger is at an end, but our disgrace will be lasting, and the month of June 1780 will ever be marked by a dark and diabolical fanaticism, which I had supposed to be extinct, but which actually subsists in Great Britain perhaps beyond any other Country in Europe" (*Letters*, II, 245).

Gibbon's real fear was not of the "forty thousand Puritans such as they might be at the time of Cromwell" but of the fanaticism, bigotry, and uncontrolled zeal which transformed reasoning man into something worse than a beast and which would deprive him of the audience to which he had so confidently addressed the rational tone of his *History*. In fact, the riots were not the beginning of a violent revolution in Great Britain; but they did herald an age which was less likely to be sympathetic to a work presented with such an appearance of order, decency, and decorum.

Volumes II and III of the *Decline and Fall* were published on March 1, 1781; and, although they were not so warmly welcomed as the first volume had been, they were better received than Gibbon's account in his *Autobiography* gives us reason to believe. Four thousand copies were printed within the year, and there was much to reassure the author in the private and public praises which he received. He thought that these volumes were more readable than the first because his writing had become more fluent, but he noticed that many purchasers were putting off the pleasure of reading them until the summer when the London season would be over and society would have retired to "dull aunts and purling brooks." He was also prepared for a less favorable reception because the excitement of novelty could only be attached to the first volume of such a series. There may, too, have been some reason in his fears that the holding of political office and the publication of the *Mémoire Justificatif* had made him unpopular with his political opponents, and no one can be in any doubt that he had attracted the hatred of some clergymen—a powerful and numerous class (he wrote in a letter to Madame Necker) which has always considered the forgiveness of injuries more as a dogma than as a precept (*Letters*, II, 263).

He was, however, generously praised by the learned, among whom were the historian William Robertson, and the economist Adam Smith; and by more private friends like Lord Hardwicke and Madame Necker he was urged to continue the *History*. The most amusing tribute of society to the work was undoubtedly that of the Duke of Gloucester who is reputed to have thanked Gibbon for a presentation copy with the words "Another damned thick, square book. Always scribble, scribble, scribble! Eh! Mr. Gibbon."[16] The variety of criticism did not deter him from continuing the *History*—"un travail qui fait le charme de ma vie" (*Letters*, II, 263)—and in the October of the same year he was discussing with Lord Hardwicke the relative interest of the Arab and Turkish parts which he had yet to write.

It was in this summer that he took a house at Brighthelmstone (as Brighton was then called), for he was able to afford this modest luxury after his election to Lymington. He was now well known, and he was thoroughly enjoying the amusements of society. If he visited the Sheffields often (Holroyd had been created Baron Sheffield of Dunamore in 1780 and hereafter appears under that name in this work), he was able to offer them some practical help by finding lodgings for them or by putting them up at Bentinck Street. In London, his friends and his clubs kept him pleasantly occupied; and he was as likely to sup with a judge and an actress as with his aunt Porten and the Sheffields (*Letters*, II, 286). In spite of occasional attacks of the gout, his was a very pleasant life; and he realized this sufficiently to enjoy it consciously.

In May, 1782, the half-expected thunderbolt fell: the Lords of Trade were abolished and with them went Gibbon's salary of seven or eight hundred pounds a year. He wrote jauntily: "Next Wednesday I conclude my forty fifth year and in spite of the changes of Kings and Ministers, I am very glad that I was born" (*Letters*, II, 294). His office was not legally terminated until July, 1782; and the salary was paid up to that date, but Gibbon knew that he could not live in London without a substantial addition to his private income, and he tried to obtain another government post through the influence of his friends and colleagues.

A year passed away, during which he remained a member of Parliament without an office of profit. It was pleasant to live in town and to work at his next volume; pleasant to have a little summer retreat up the Thames River at Hampton Court; pleasant to flatten obtuse critics like Joseph Priestley; pleasant to watch Mrs Siddons acting; and pleasant to admire the real merit of the Younger Pitt in Parliament— but all these pleasures could not be enjoyed without money; and Gibbon had no doubt about what he wanted most of all to do. In August, 1782, he wrote to his stepmother: "My private life is a gentle and not unpleasing continuation of my old labours, and I am again involved as I shall be for some years in the decline and fall of the Roman Empire. Some fame, some profit, and the assurance of daily amusement encourage me to persist" (*Letters*, II, 305–306). His chief pleasure was the composition of the *History*. The year after the dissolution of the Board of Trade was spent in studying the age of Justinian, and the fourth volume of the *History* was almost complete in July, 1783.

By May, 1783, it seemed obvious that no government office would ever again be offered to him. Recent reforms had halved the number of places at the disposal of ministers and had doubled the number of applicants for them. Gibbon was at last driven to do what he had so often meditated with pleasure: to propose to his old friend Deyverdun that they should set up a joint household in Lausanne, or at least set up adjoining apartments. He had chosen a happy moment for the proposal: some friends of Deyverdun who had been sharing his house were about to leave; the place was free, and he was delighted with the scheme.

IV *Lausanne*

On September 17, 1783, Gibbon sailed for France; and ten days later he was in Lausanne. The satisfaction of meeting and conversing with Deyverdun was alone worth a journey of six hundred miles; his sincere, tender, and sensible friend (*Letters*, II, 376) had indeed provided the ideal home for a philosophical historian. All Gibbon's letters rejoice in the exchange of London for Lausanne, and his happiness there seems to have been unalloyed during his friend's lifetime: "perhaps two persons so perfectly fitted for each other were never created by Nature and education" (*Letters*, II, 387).

His new routine was simple: he rose each day at eight, breakfasted at nine in the English manner with his English man servant in attendance, spent the morning in his study, and dined with Deyverdun at two. After dinner and the departure of any visitors, the two men read together, played chess, retired to their studies, went visiting, or spent an hour at the coffee house. In the evening, they went out to play whist with friends and retired home to sup on bread and cheese between nine and ten. Gibbon was often persuaded into staying out later at private and numerous suppers since he had rapidly become a general favorite. Six months of residence were enough to reassure him that a capital and a crowd might contain much less real society than the small circle of his gentle retirement (*Letters*, II, 406); and by June, 1784, he had seriously resumed the progress of his *History* (*Letters*, II, 412). He expected it to take him some three or four years longer, and for that time indeed he was happily settled in Lausanne, troubled only by an occasional fit of the gout and by the winding up of money matters relating to the sale of the family estate of Lenborough. In the interests of domestic comfort, Gibbon and Deyverdun seriously discussed the possibility of marriage for one of them; but Gibbon had long since declared three other interests which precluded matrimony—his friendship with Deyverdun, his "passion for his wife or mistress (Fanny Lausanne)," and his constant preoccupation with his other wife—the decline and fall of the Roman Empire (*Letters*, III, 12, 32, 44).

One event only (apart from his perpetual money worries) which occurred in England during his absence caused him real concern, the death of his aunt Kitty. A part of his reply to Lord Sheffield's letter of condolence has already been quoted in another context; a few additional sentences show how deep his attachment to her had been: "an intercourse of thirty years endeared her to me as the faithful friend and the agreable companion; you have seen with what freedom and confidence we lived together, and have often admired her character and conversation which could alike please the young and the old. All this is now lost, finally irrecoverably lost! I will agree with Mylady that the immortality of the soul is, on some occasions a very comfortable doctrine" (*Letters,* III, 46). This, one of Gibbon's few private references to the consolations of religion, marks the depth of his grief and the sincerity of his self-reproaches.

In such afflicting circumstances the *History* was a resource indeed; but, since it was not getting along fast enough, he had found it necessary to devote his evenings as well as his mornings to its completion. Moreover, he could now compute how many pages he still had to write and almost how many days he would yet need for writing them; and in January, 1787, he was assured that he could bring the completed *History*, entirely revised and with its notes correct, to London for printing no later than August, 1787 (*Letters*, III, 60). It was, in fact, in June that the work was completed; and it is again to Gibbon himself that we must turn for an account of his feelings on that memorable occasion: he recalls in the *Autobiography* that he had recorded the moment of conception in Rome and continues:

I shall now commemorate the hour of my final deliverance. It was on the day, or rather night, of the 27th of June, 1787, between the hours of eleven and twelve, that I wrote the last lines of the last page, in a summerhouse in my garden. After laying down my pen, I took several turns in a *berceau*, or covered walk of acacias, which commands a prospect of the country, the lake, and the mountains. The air was temperate, the sky was serene, the silver orb of the moon was reflected from the waters, and all nature was silent. I will not dissemble the first emotions of joy on recovery of my freedom, and, perhaps, the establishment of my fame. But my pride was soon humbled, and a sober melancholy was soon spread over my mind, by the idea that I had taken an everlasting leave of an old and agreeable companion, and that whatsoever might be the future date of my *History*, the life of the historian must be short and precarious (205).

This fit of elegantly appropriate melancholy did not last long, for there were immediate practical steps to be taken.

He spent almost a year in England, supervising the publication of his *History* and visiting his friends. Preparation of the elaborate quartos took up much of the first eight months. Though he was justly proud of the fact that his first rough manuscript, without any intermediate copy, had been sent to the press, there was still work to be done. Proof sheets were sent to him at Sheffield Place as they were prepared, and he must have corrected between twenty-four and thirty-six pages every week from the middle of August to the end of March. He was pleased to find himself remembered by polite society; and he made a point of visiting his former patron, Lord North, who was now wholly blind. Some of the debt of gratitude which he felt was repaid by his dedication of the last volumes to that statesman when North no longer had any power to confer favors upon Gibbon.

The highlight of Gibbon's year in England should have been and very probably was his fifty-first birthday. The *History* had been ready at the end of March but publication was put off until May 8 so that both events could be celebrated at a dinner given by his friend and publisher,

Thomas Cadell. A happy occasion, it was dignified by the recitation of an ode to the historian after dinner. One of William Hayley's stanzas alone would have satisfied the vainest of men. The poem urges England to rejoice over the fame of her great men in the following terms:

> Science for thee a *Newton* rais'd;
> For thy renown a *Shakespeare* blaz'd,
>   Lord of the drama's sphere!
> In different Fields to equal Praise
> See Hist'ry now thy Gibbon raise
>   To shine with a Peer!

To his stepmother, he wrote: "I feel as if a mountain was removed from my breast." Lord North, his former political patron and friend; Robertson, the Scottish historian whom he respected; and Adam Smith, the economist, all wrote of their lively satisfaction with the new volumes; and Gibbon was present in the House of Commons to hear a flattering tribute from Richard Brinsley Sheridan, when he charged Warren Hastings with crimes that "were unparalleled in atrociousness . . . nothing equal in criminality was to be traced either in ancient or modern history in the correct pages of Tacitus or the luminous pages of Gibbon."[17] C. W. von Riemberg, the German translator of the *History*, said that everyone in Britain spoke of the appearance of the last three volumes as of the completion of some work of national importance.[18]

By the end of June, Gibbon's arrangements for departure were almost complete. His old servant Caplen (who had attended him again while he was in London) had packed the remainder of his library in seven crates for transmission to Lausanne; his social round was completed by splendid and memorable dinners with Warren Hastings and the Prince of Wales, both of whom had asked to meet him; and he went to Sheffield Place to await the return of a young Swiss friend, Wilhelm de Sévery, from his last sightseeing trips to Stowe. Gibbon took the opportunity of writing to his cousin (now Baron Eliot) a letter of civil compliment, and to his aunt Hester—"the Northamptonshire saint"—a letter to which we owe one of the most interesting statements of his religious opinions. It may have been mere policy in the hope of inheritance which induced him to write to her that "I can assure you with truth, that I consider Religion as the best guide of youth and the best support of old age: that I firmly believe there is less real happiness in the business and pleasures of the world, than in the life, which you have chosen, of devotion and retirement" (*Letters*, III, 118). It may be, too, that he has specifically omitted maturity and middle age from the enjoyment of religious consolation, but the statement is a confession of a moderate faith wholly consistent with his major writings.

He left Dover on July 21 and arrived back at his own house in Lausanne in time for dinner on July 30, ready to take up his pleasant social life among a group of sincere friends and admirers—free at last from the agreeable fatigues of authorship. How happy he was his letters home attest in a great variety of ways. On October 4 he wrote to Lord Sheffield: "After having been so long chained to the oar in a splendid galley indeed, I freely and fairly enjoy my liberty as I promised in my preface, range without controul over the wide expanse of my library, converse, as my fancy prompts me with poets and historians, philosophers and Orators of every age and language, and often indulge my meditations in the invention and arrangement of mighty works which I shall probably never find time or application to execute" (*Letters*, III, 131).

The warm satisfaction of returning to his own house, his own library, and his own garden was somewhat lessened by apprehensions about the health of Deyverdun; and, when his friend was seized by a violent stroke in September, it became clear that he had not long to live. During the whole of the first year of his return to Lausanne, all Gibbon's pleasures were overshadowed by this consciousness. After a protracted illness, Deyverdun died on July 4, 1789, at Aix-les-Bains, where he had gone to take the waters. Gibbon sought consolation in the thought that death had prevented a premature old age and a prolonged period of decaying faculties; but after thirty-three years of friendship—and in particular after the five years of happy and tranquil life together at La Grotte—it was not possible for reason to assuage or to repress his heartfelt grief. It was nearly ten days before he could write of his loss even to Lord Sheffield: "I want to change the scene; and beautiful as the garden and prospect must appear to every eye, I feel that the state of my own mind casts a gloom over them; every spot, every walk every bench recalls the memory of those hours, of those conversations which will return no more" (*Letters*, III, 163).

V   *Alone*

The melancholy sense of solitude which Gibbon now felt in Lausanne made him consider the possibility of a return to the neighborhood of his English friends, but he was deterred from taking such a major step by the presence of his Swiss friends the Séverys; by the enormous trouble and expense of a move; and by his possession of La Grotte. It was probably this last factor which most helped him to make up his mind to stay; for by the terms of Deyverdun's will, Gibbon was able to retain possession of the house for his life on easy terms; and this he eventually resolved to do, but he still felt acutely lonely and looked for someone with whom he could wish to share his home. The companionship of his young relative Charlotte Porten and even the desperate expedient of marriage were considered as possible means of alleviating his solitary misery. However, he had no particular lady in mind, he was not in love with any of the "hyaenas of Lausanne," and his first desolation gradually subsided under the influence of a routine which absorbed him ever more into the daily life of the Sévery family.

The disordered state of his own affairs seemed to him to be reflected in the revolutions going on around him. The day he wrote to Sheffield of Deyverdun's death was the day on which the Bastille fell and the French Revolution began. Even the Swiss canton of Berne, in which Lausanne is situated, was going through a troubled period; and the neighboring city of Geneva came increasingly under the domination of French revolutionary ideas and eventually of the French armies. Gibbon's correspondence from this time until the end of his life is full of pejorative references to the spirit and effects of democracy and democratical principles "which lead by a path of flowers into the Abyss of Hell" (*Letters*, III, 268). Against this background he began to appreciate the stability of England as the last refuge of liberty and law. "What would you have me say of the affairs of France?" he wrote to Sheffield in December, 1789; and he replied to his own question: "The abuses of the court and government called aloud for reformation. . . . If they had been content with a liberal translation of our system, if they had respected the prerogatives of the crown and the privileges of the Nobles, they might have raised a solid fabric on the only true foundation the natural Aristocracy of a great Country. How different is the prospect!" (*Letters,* III, 183–84). The Gordon Riots had appeared evil and visionary enough to Gibbon in the 1780s, but the new Revolution upset all his cherished feelings and convictions about the value of reason and about the inevitability of progress. Only England and Switzerland were, for the moment, happy countries.

Gibbon thought about several new works in his renewed retirement from England, and he even confided to friends and acquaintances his various projects. His first idea was to write a work on the origins of the House of Brunswick, which would have had great topical interest for the British since George III was the third monarch of that German royal house to reign in England. All that remains of this project is the eighty introductory pages which were printed posthumously in the *Miscellaneous Works*. Had the essay been completed, it would have been the first in a series of *Historical Excursions* into unusual or little-known territories, which were likely to have been every bit as entertaining and instructive as the great *History* itself (*Letters*, III, 202–206). He wrote to Cadell to propose a seventh volume for the *Decline and Fall*—a supplement including additional notes, maps, and a critical review of his authorities—but he did not even start it. He must, however, have written at this time the essay on *The Position of the Meridional Line*, which was published posthumously; and he was certainly writing and rewriting the *Memoirs* of his own life and works which are referred to as the *Autobiography*.

After the melancholy excitement of straightening out his own and Deyverdun's affairs in the autumn and winter of 1789–90, Gibbon was seized by a severe and prolonged attack of gout, which made him all the more grateful for the society of Lausanne, and helped him to reestablish himself in it, because cheerful visits and parties had to come to him to beguile him of his pains. For five months his painful confinement to his house was "softened by books, by the possession of every comfort and convenience, by a succession, each evening, of agreable company, and by a flow of equal spirits and general good health" (*Letters*, III, 197). Shortly after his recovery, the death of his aunt Hester Gibbon left him with a handsome inheritance in Sussex. Perhaps this restoration of health and of hope encouraged him to begin the two projects of the autumn of 1790 already referred to—the *Antiquities of the House of Brunswick* and the seventh volume of the *Decline and Fall*. These were again interrupted by ill health at the beginning of 1791, when he was confined to his bedroom for two months.

With Gibbon's renewed health, gaiety returned to La Grotte: on March 29, he gave a ball. The domestic details were managed for him by the young Séverys, and their grateful friend found good all that they had done for him. As he wrote to Lord Sheffield afterwards: "the assembly of men and women was pleased and pleasing, the music good, the illumination splendid, the refreshments profuse" (*Letters*, III, 219). Gibbon was present at the supper laid for one hundred and thirty; but he stole away to bed at two, for his legs were still weak as a result of his illness. The ball was concluded for him at seven in the morning by

Wilhelm de Sévery and his sister Angletine. This was an exceptional festivity, but he gave frequent dinner parties and looked forward to holding his customary Sunday evening assemblies in the summer.

His cheerful accounts of himself in the letters of this period were designed to recommend the liveliness of Lausanne to the Sheffields, with the deliberate intention of inducing them to visit him there. They were persuaded at last in 1791, and they reached Lausanne on July 23 after an exciting journey through revolutionary France. La Grotte and Lausanne seemed very tame in comparison, and the lively Maria was very much surprised that her father's friend should have been content to exchange the excitements of English society for the flat tranquility of Swiss life, but her impression was soon modified by the friendliness and kindness of the Sévery family. Trips from Lausanne to see the Neckers at Copet and the scenery of the Mont Blanc massif were altogether delightful.

During the rest of the two months which they spent at Lausanne, the Sheffields got to know all Gibbon's friends as well as a large number of the exiled French. There were plenty of opportunities, for there were parties every evening, at which, if Maria is to be believed, Gibbon was always the central figure. According to her "when the 'King of the Place' as he is called, opens his mouth (which you know he generally does some time before he has arranged his sentence) all wait in awful and respectful silence for what shall follow and look up to it as an Oracle."[19] There is some reason to believe this description, for, when the Sheffields came to read his *Memoirs* to the family circle in 1794, they sounded just like his ordinary conversational style.

Maria's keen satirical wit may have found much to exercise it in Gibbon himself and in his Swiss friends, but it was very much modified by the variety of company which the Sheffields enjoyed and by the real friendship of many of the Swiss. When they left at the beginning of October, Gibbon missed them very much and sought consolation elsewhere. He visited the Neckers at the end of February, 1792, and he was made as comfortable as if he had been in his own home. As a result of this visit, he and Suzanne began writing to each other again with something of the warmth of their very first correspondence. In one of the letters of this period, Suzanne declares that he had never for an instant ceased to be the object of her admiration and of that tender and pure affection over which time itself could have no empire.[20] Gibbon was sufficiently moved to write to her as his first and last love, and she found herself unable to decide which of the two titles was the more pleasing to her.[21] In late middle age he turned with gratitude and with real emotion to renew the most deeply felt and the longest-enduring of his youthful ties.

In the course of the year, Gibbon was agitated by the successes of the French armies; by the revolution in Geneva; by his apprehensions for Salomon de Sévery's health; by his fears for the safety of Wilhelm who had gone to serve in the army; and by some disquiet over his own bodily state. He had hoped to visit England in 1792, and there is in the letters one hint of an obstacle which was beginning to give Gibbon some concern when he writes casually of the difficulty of transporting so unwieldy and inactive a being as himself. He had suffered not only from gout, but also from a hydrocele or collection of water, which he would never allow anyone to refer to although it gave him a curiously and conspicuously portly figure. He had consulted a doctor about it while he was in the militia, but he had apparently done nothing about it in all the thirty years since.[22] The discomfort of traveling in such a state could clearly be considerable, and his consciousness of this factor may have contributed to his unusual gloom. It was unlike him to write to his friends of being so agitated that he could not read or think, but such was his state at the end of 1792. He wrote to Wilhelm, a sentence which was designed to inure him to the idea of his father's death: "Life is only a struggle, more or less drawn out, against physical ills which attack us from all sides and as we advance along the road the struggle becomes more painful and unequal."[23] Such language speaks eloquently of his own feelings, and it anticipates the two serious events of 1793 which at last precipitated him into action and which may have hastened his own death.

On January 29, 1793, Salomon de Sévery died. For all Gibbon's philosophical anticipations, this death was a real grief to him. He hurried from a visit to the Neckers at Rolle to console the widow and children, but he felt that his happy circle was breaking up around him and that ties which had so long bound him to Lausanne were loosening. The second blow was the sudden and unexpected death of Lady Sheffield in London on April 3. Gibbon at once made arrangements to go to England to console Lord Sheffield. He arrived at Dover on June 2 and went straight to Sheffield Place, only to find that business, company, and other amusements were helping Sheffield to recover so rapidly that he was already looking round for a second wife.

Gibbon paid many visits both with the Sheffields and alone to old and new friends. On October 9 he visited Mrs. Gibbon at Bath, who had just recovered from a severe illness; but he found her just the same as she had been twenty years before, talking of living to be ninety; and they both enjoyed the ten days which he spent almost exclusively in her society. On his way back to London, he stayed at Althorpe with Lord and Lady Spencer whom he had met in Lausanne; and he seemed as cheerful and as unconcerned as he had ever been, thoroughly enjoying his reintroduction to English society.

On November 8, however, he complained in a letter to Lord Sheffield of fatigue and of feeling unwell, and in another letter on the following day he spoke of seeking medical advice, although he intended to dine with Lord and Lady Lucan that afternoon. Only on the eleventh did he reveal to his friend the unpleasant necessity of tapping the hydrocele which he had so long neglected. The operation was delayed until November 14, so that Lord Sheffield could be present to support his friend. A few hours before it took place, Gibbon wrote at length in his usual cheerful manner to Wilhelm de Sévery, describing the new carriage that was being built for him, discussing the Sévery investments, and accounting for his failure to find suitable employment for Wilhelm as a tutor and traveling companion. Nothing is more characteristic of him than the apparent stoicism and cheerfulness with which he faced his physical difficulties. Five days later he wrote again of the success of the operation, but the note was written in such a trembling hand that it alarmed his friends in Lausanne.

On the advice of his physicians, Gibbon continued to lead a normal life, and a second operation on November 24 left him equally cheerful and expectant of a radical cure. He dined several times with Lord Loughborough in early December, and he seems to have been seeking political office or an English peerage from Lord Sheffield before he went down to Sheffield Place for Christmas on the tenth. Until Christmas, Gibbon seemed well, although suffering some discomfort; but after-wards his condition deteriorated so alarmingly that he could hardly move about to enjoy the company of the Sheffields' guests, and he felt compelled to return to London to consult his doctors on January 5, 1794. The journey was a very trying and exhausting one, and Lord Sheffield hastened to town after him. On the thirteenth he submitted to another operation, which was thought to have been successful. Lord Sheffield returned home on the fourteenth and Gibbon received several visitors, including Lady Lucan, Lady Spencer, Madame da Silva, and Mr. Crauford with whom he had dined so recently: "They talked, as usual, on various subjects; and . . . Mr. Gibbon happened to fall into a conversation, not uncommon with him, on the probable duration of his life. He said, that he thought himself a good life for ten, twelve, or perhaps twenty years."[24] The next day he was dead.

CHAPTER 2

The Decline and Fall

I   *"A Cubic Foot of Reading Matter"*

"SHALL I be accused of vanity, if I add that a monument is superfluous?" Gibbon asked in his will. To this rhetorical question about his posthumous fame, we have no difficulty in giving the correct answer. *The Decline and Fall of the Roman Empire* is itself a truly monumental work. We may read it in the six quarto volumes of the original edition (almost a cubic foot of reading matter), or in the eight volumes of the great nineteenth-century issue re-edited by Dr. William Smith from the edition of Dean Milman, or in the seven volumes of the scholarly edition by J. B. Bury, printed at the beginning of the present century. Monuments are the resource of antiquaries, but Gibbon's *History* is no mere antique: it is still very much alive as history, and it is instinct with the principles of eighteenth-century decorum and humanity.

Hugh Trevor-Roper rightly calls Gibbon "the greatest of the historians of the Enlightenment, the only one of them who is still read not only as a stylist, but also as a historian." His *History* has survived the test of nearly two hundred years of appreciation and appraisal because the ordering of its subject matter, as well as the immortal affectation of his unique manner (the phrase is Bury's), conveys a view of life and implies a constant evaluation of the events as they are related. If we ask what the *History* is about, we cannot do better than examine Gibbon's claim that the work describes the triumph of barbarism and religion—an epigram that explains one of the main sources of Gibbon's fame and notoriety. He seemed to many of his contemporaries to be implying a causal relationship: they inferred that the historian meant them to believe that it was the triumph of Christianity which led to the fall of Rome and the coming of the Dark Ages. There are many such suggestions in the *History*, but this implication is not its main substance. It does exactly what it set out to do: namely, narrates the history of the decline and fall of the Roman

Empire, indicates the causes of that decline, and pictures the ways in which the fall has shaped modern Europe. Just so long as we recognize the importance of our Roman heritage, Gibbon's description of it will continue to command our attention.

The original plan of the whole *History* is laid out in the author's preface to the first volume. He had divided some thirteen centuries of Roman history into three periods which he intended to treat at similar length. The first period lasted from the Age of Trajan and the Antonines to the capture of Rome by the Goths—a period of some four centuries, from A.D. 100 to 500. The second period started with the reign of Justinian and the restoration of the Eastern Empire and lasted until the rise of Mahomet and of Charlemagne—a period of another three centuries from 500 to 814. The third and final period stretched from the revival of the Western Empire to the taking of Constantinople by the Turks—a period of some six and a half centuries, from 815 to 1453.

We can see that what interested Gibbon most was the earliest period, for he gave three of the original six quarto volumes to it. When he had finished his first volume, he thought, as we have observed, that one additional volume would bring him to the sixth century, but, in fact, he needed three volumes in which to do this first period justice. Consequently, the remaining two historical periods—nearly a thousand years of history—were compressed into the last three volumes. J. B. Bury maintained that this mode of dealing with the subject was in harmony with the author's contemptuous attitude to the Byzantine or Eastern Empire, and there can be no doubt that ignorance (occasioned by a lack of available historical materials) influenced Gibbon's view of Byzantium. On his main subject, however—the Western Empire—he is ample, impartial and entertaining. Each of the first three volumes of the *History* forms such a very readable whole that it will be convenient to describe them separately, while remembering that they are all part of the same complex narrative.

If we had only the first volume of the work, it would still be recognized for the masterpiece it is. The narrative works carefully up to a climax in the last two chapters, and it holds our attention because of the skill with which facts are ordered and marshaled. The story is frequently interrupted in order to introduce essential qualifications and themes, to highlight a main idea by a contrast of historical personalities, or to tell us about the manners and laws of foreign nations; and these interpolations introduce variety and create a satisfying pattern of historical interrelationship without the reader's noticing the art which stimulates his interest and satisfies his curiosity. The ease and grace of the writing and the compression and inclusiveness of the matter are equally the products of laborious research and of careful revision. Gibbon was to write later that he made many experiments before he could "hit the middle tone between a dull chronicle and a rhetorical declamation" (*Autobiography*, 177). In fact, he wrote the first chapter three times and the second and third chapters twice before he was moderately satisfied with their effect. The unity of the *History* is imposed by a style which takes its root from a philosophical view of life, and the reader is induced by the seductions of the style to share the historian's convictions.

The truth of this statement is illustrated by the opening paragraph of the *History*, which speaks with the voice of authority and with the assurance of knowledge. This paragraph admirably exemplifies the style and also gives a brief abstract of the matter of the first volume:[1]

In the second century of the Christian Era, the empire of Rome comprehended the fairest part of the earth, and the most civilised portion of mankind. The frontiers of that extensive monarchy were guarded by ancient renown and disciplined valour. The gentle, but powerful, influence of laws and manners had gradually cemented the union of the provinces. Their peaceful inhabitants enjoyed and abused the advantages of wealth and luxury. The image of a free constitution was preserved with decent reverence: the Roman senate appeared to possess the sovereign authority, and devolved on the emperors all the executive powers of government. During a happy period of more than fourscore years the public administration was conducted by the virtue and abilities of Nerva, Trajan, Hadrian and the two Antonines. It is the design of this, and of the two succeeding chapters, to describe the prosperous condition of their empire; and afterwards, from the death of Marcus Antoninus, to deduce the most important circumstances of its decline and fall: a revolution which will ever be remembered, and is still felt by the nations of the earth.

Like a good storyteller, Gibbon plunges us into the middle of his subject, and the balance of the last two clauses of the first sentence reminds us that antithesis, or the careful presentation of opposing evidences, is an eighteenth-century habit of thought. So also is the substitution of the abstract for the concrete in the next sentence—we should be more likely to say "brave and obedient soldiers" than "disciplined valour."

Gibbon's more insidious skills are evidenced in the pairing of "enjoyed and abused" as though, in Rome at least, it were impossible for pleasure to avoid falling into extravagance: the luxury of which he accuses the Romans has sinister overtones. His longer central sentence foreshadows one of the main causes of the decline of the Empire: the forms of freedom were kept while the emperors slowly but surely acquired despotic powers. The smoothness of the prose matches the insidiousness of the process which is described. The fact that the first emperors were virtuous and able effectively masks the degeneration of the Empire, and the dangers of despotism are only felt by the reader in the sudden serious sonorousness of the last two clauses of the paragraph: the Roman decline is indeed a "revolution which will ever be remembered, and is still felt by the nations of the earth."

In accordance with this introduction, the opening three chapters give a picture of the Empire as it was before its decline set in—a picture of "the period in the history of the world during which the condition of the human race was most happy and prosperous." While Gibbon dilates upon the happiness of this relatively brief period, he makes his readers aware of its precarious nature. The Empire had been built in the frugal days of the republic: with the coming of prosperity, republican virtue declined. The vast increase in the size of the Empire made democratic government impossible, while the growth of monarchy curtailed individual rights and personal freedom. The conduct of the early emperors may have been virtuous but the institution of absolute monarchy carried within itself the seeds of its own decay. This important message of the whole history is endlessly repeated but with fascinating individual variations in each separate historical example.

Then, with a fine sense of historical perspective, Gibbon notes the changes which have overtaken the country around Rome within the space of a thousand years or so: "On that celebrated ground the first consuls deserved triumphs, their successors adorned villas, and *their* posterity have erected convents." Valor was replaced by villas, personal virtue by luxurious self-indulgence, and men were willingly self-deceived as long as they could be comfortable. The historian's reflection establishes the fact that human frailties account for the early establishment of despotism, and he illustrates this fact in Roman history: when Augustus had successfully acquired the exercise of supreme power, he found that "the senate and people would submit to slavery, provided they were respectfully assured that they still enjoyed their ancient freedom." At the moment of Rome's highest prosperity, therefore, Augustus was able to establish an absolute monarchy by disguising it in the forms of a commonwealth. For the rational freedom of the republic the Romans were happy to substitute the luxury and the vices which flourish under tyranny. Such, in substance, is the main thesis of the first chapters in which the virtues of the Antonines only provide a brief and illuminating contrast with the lurid vices of succeeding emperors.

The next four chapters reveal a slow, steady descent from the virtues of this ephemeral golden age. The murder of the vicious Commodus, the assassination of the virtuous Pertinax, and the auction of the Empire by the Praetorian Guard to the highest bidder, Julian, are the preface to the abolition of even the forms of republican government in the reign of Severus. A note of foreboding had been struck when it was said that Augustus had been elected by the authority of the senate and with the consent of the soldiers: the army comes to assume an ever more sinister and powerful role in the election of succeeding emperors. In the case of the unfortunate Julian, the new emperor was betrayed by the guard which had elevated him; and, on the accession of Severus (whose bribes were larger), Julian "was conducted into a private apartment of the baths of the palace and beheaded as a common criminal, after having purchased with an immense treasure, an anxious and precarious reign of only sixty-six days." Such are the ironies of history and the extremes of human folly as seen through the eyes of Gibbon.

The falsehood and insincerity of a tyrant are admirably suggested by the language which Gibbon uses to describe the manner of Lucius Septimus Severus as he pronounced the funeral oration over his virtuous predecessor, Pertinax. He spoke "with studied eloquence, inward satisfaction, and well-acted sorrow." This capacity for dissimulation augured well for the success of the new emperor, but the melancholy events of his reign mark that decline of the Roman spirit which was the real cause of the ultimate disaster. His successful campaigns against two rivals, Clodius Albinus in Gaul, and Pescennius Niger in Syria, united the Empire; but his cruel despotism in crushing republican freedoms gave him an active share in procuring the decline of his empire. The tyranny of his son Caracalla (who murdered his brother Geta) and the licentious follies of Elagabalus were succeeded by the wise administration which was carried on under the name of his cousin, Alexander Severus, by his mother and his grandmother; but an acceleration of the process of decline may be deduced from Gibbon's brief chapter headings which speak of cruelty, follies, murder, relaxation of discipline, and assassination. As a fair example, Chapter VII tells of the elevation and tyranny of Maximin, of rebellion in Africa and Italy, of civil wars and seditions, of violent deaths, and of the usurpation of Philip. Like Mr. Boffin, we may be astonished to find so many "scarers" in print.

At the end of Chapter VII, the plain chronological narrative of Roman history breaks off; and, taking Tacitus as his model, Gibbon relieves the attention of the reader from a uniform scene of vice and misery by indulging himself in a description of Persian and of German manners and customs. A masterly interruption, it gives to the reader in the succeeding narrative a sense of the armies which "threatened as an impending cloud the . . . provinces of the declining empire of Rome" and which were soon to make inroads upon it. At the same time, it provides a sprightly and entertaining digression. The German chapter dwells upon the crude settlements of that people, their domestic virtue, and the rude energy which was to enable them to triumph over the Romans. The Persian chapter relates with speed and economy the circumstances surrounding the brief revival of the Persian Empire under Artaxerxes, and it elaborates two of the most important themes of the *Decline and Fall.*

The first theme Gibbon has already dwelt upon at length: the Persians are shown to be in as much danger from their own luxury, indiscipline, and corruption as are the Romans. They are suffering from the universally enervating effect of too much prosperity and from the evils of despotism, at the very moment when they are ready to precipitate the fall of the Roman Empire in the east. The second theme is sounded for the first time here, and it concerns religion. Gibbon notes that Roman greatness owed much to universal religious toleration (we have remarked the supersession of villas by convents in the Campagna), but the account in this chapter of the re-establishment of the Magian cult by Artaxerxes is Gibbon's first venture into the history of religion. It produces some of his finest comic irony. In one entertaining paragraph he equates religion with inspiration and enthusiasm; and he shows us that, when indulged, these qualities produce self-deception and imposture. In a way familiar to the eighteenth century, he suggests, without affirming, that the Magian tenets were founded on fraud—a pious fraud perhaps, but nonetheless a fraud.

Gibbon's attack is so characteristic of his method that we must pause for a moment to see what happened when the Persian king called a religious council to determine and formulate Magian doctrine:

> To suppress the idolaters, reunite the schismatics, and confute the unbelievers by the infallible decision of a general council, the pious Artaxerxes summoned the Magi from all parts of his dominions. These priests, who had so long sighed in contempt and obscurity, obeyed the welcome summons; and on the appointed day appeared to the number of about eighty thousand. But as the debates of so tumultuous an assembly could not have been directed by the authority of reason, or influenced by the art of policy, the Persian synod was reduced, by successive operations, to forty thousand, to four thousand, to four hundred, to forty, and at last to seven Magi, the most respected for their learning and piety. One of these, Erdaviraph, a young but holy prelate, received from the hands of his brethren three cups of soporiferous wine. He drank them off, and instantly fell into a long and profound sleep. As soon as he waked he related to the king and to the believing multitude his journey to Heaven, and his intimate conferences with the Deity. Every doubt was silenced by this supernatural evidence; and the articles of the faith of Zoroaster were fixed with equal authority and precision.

This paragraph forms a useful contrast to the opening paragraph of the *History*, cited earlier, since the historian has laid in every sentence of this one a trap of irony or of innuendo for the simple or the credulous enthusiast. In the first sentence, the king is called "pious"; but there is some doubt whether his summons to the Magi is an act of policy or of devotion. Gibbon's use of the adjective in the context of the sentence creates doubts about the accuracy of its application. Moreover, the phrase "infallible decisions of a general council" can only pass without comment until we know what the decisions were and how sensible they were. The episode shows them to be the product of "inspiration" and therefore untrustworthy. We are invited to infer that the priests were worldly, since they had sighed in contempt and obscurity and had found the summons into the world of politics welcome.

The narrator's tone of respectful humility seems to be renewed in the next sentence, but in fact it is even more ironic in its innuendos. Must an assembly of priests be tumultuous? Does the author expect any such assembly to be reasonable? Whose policy or cunning was likely to influence the assembly? Such are the questions which the sentence is designed to raise in the reader's mind. Even if we could take the sentence entirely at its face value and respect the "learning and piety" of the seven Magi, the anecdote of Erdaviraph's vision is intended to spring the largest trap and to remove all possibility of reverence for inspiration from the most credulous mind. Gibbon does not need to *say* that the tenets of the Zoroastrian faith had been fixed by the ravings of a drunkard, for his paragraph implies all this and a great deal more. The tone of the paragraph tells us what value is to be attached to supernatural evidence and makes us realize that the "authority and precision" with which the articles of faith are fixed are "equal" only in their unreliability. Reread in the light of this knowledge, the paragraph can be seen for the masterpiece of comedy that it is, and will be recognized as the first of Gibbon's attacks upon unreason in religion.

The two interchapters on Persia and Germany provide, then, not only important historical information but also a superior kind of light relief. The reader returns, enlightened and amused, to take up the main thread of Gibbon's narrative where he had left it, in doubt whether the usurpation of Philip would be successful or not. It was not. The general irruption of the barbarians (for which the interchapters have prepared us), several new emperors, and twenty years of shame and misfortune provide the substance of Chapter X. One emperor in this chapter did see that the cause of decline lay in the loss of public virtue and in the maladministration of the laws; and he attempted, vainly, to reform these abuses. The neat antitheses of his epitaph show how impossible a task lay before any reforming emperor: "It was easier to vanquish the Goths than to eradicate the public vices, yet even in the first of these enterprises, Decius lost his army and his life."

This horrid picture of universal disorder is balanced by a succeeding chapter of triumphs. As Gibbon put it, "The removal of an effeminate tyrant made way for a succession of heroes"; and the successes of the emperors Claudius and Aurelian restore for a single chapter the glory of the Roman name. But the death of Aurelian was followed by another period of barbarian invasions and by the peaceful but dangerous establishment of some thousands of the barbarians within the Empire. The failure of several minor emperors to prevent this nibbling away at the fringes of the Empire occupies another chapter after which, by that law of contrasts which appears to guide Gibbon's composition of the *History*, the thirteenth chapter is devoted to the twenty years of prosperity and comparative tranquility enjoyed by the Empire under Diocletian and his associates, amongst whom was Constantius, the father of Constantine.

This series of interrelated contrasts is designed to lead gradually to the important and hitherto unsuspected climax of the first volume. The substantial success of Diocletian is followed by the even greater successes of Constantine. Chapter XIV shows how, over a period of nineteen years, Constantine made conquests which amply attest the moderation of the man and the brilliance of his progress. Gradually his rivals are overcome, the Empire is reunited, the frontiers are secured against danger, and there seems to be cause for nothing but admiration. However, Gibbon has another purpose in mind which makes him wish to present Constantine as something less than admirable. He became the first Christian emperor: Christians are as prone to enthusiasm as other devout persons; enthusiasm is dangerous; the emperor's motives must, therefore, be made to appear suspect.

The process is begun by suggesting rather than stating that the emperor was an astute politician and a cunning man. His mind is said to be engrossed by carefully concealed ambition, and we are made to feel that it is artfulness which enabled him to succeed. Gibbon has so often castigated the failures of weaker emperors that this barrage of innuendo directed against the successes of Constantine should make us suspect the historian's impartiality. We are told, for example, that the virtues of Constantine were rendered more illustrious by contrast with the vices of Maxentius; or we are told that the emperor's ambition was restrained "by considerations of prudence rather than by principles of justice." This method of defaming character by inference is used consistently to neutralize the effect upon the reader of the many proofs of Constantine's valor, intelligence, probity, and abilities.

The last paragraph of the chapter continues and explains the reasons for the innuendo: "The successive steps of the elevation of Constantine . . . have been related with some minuteness and precision, not only as the events are in themselves both interesting and important, but still more as they contributed to the decline of the empire by the expense of blood and treasure, and by the perpetual increase, as well of the taxes as of the military establishment. The foundation of Constantinople, and the establishment of the Christian religion, were the immediate and memorable consequences of this revolution."

Here we have one of the most outstanding of the emperors blamed for initiating the decline of the Empire (although we have seen that decline had set in long before) and for establishing the new religion, as though the one were a direct cause or result of the other. Gibbon defers his account of the foundation of Constantinople and the Eastern Empire to a new volume: his description of the establishment of the

Christian religion forms the long and splendid peroration to the first volume, and it needs a section to itself.

II   *The Attack upon Christianity*

Gibbon was obliged to devote meticulous care and attention to the fifteenth and sixteenth chapters of his *History* because he was concerned with the history of the Christian religion. In the eighteenth century there were heavy legal penalties on the statute book for those baptized Christians who denied the truth of their faith. The historian was, therefore, in considerable difficulty: he wished to be rational in his description of the rise of Christianity, but he feared to treat the history of Christianity as he would treat any other kind of history in case he exposed himself to penalties. In using irony to help him out of this difficulty he is using a method approved by the practice of the greatest names of his age, including the object of his sincerest admiration, Hume, and of his pet aversion, Voltaire. The subject was so attractive to him that he wrote at great length and found it necessary to reduce his two chapters "by three successive revisals from a large volume to their present size" (*Autobiography*, 177). The plan was so meticulous and so brilliantly executed, and it has always excited so much feeling, that any consideration of the *History* must devote the most careful thought and attention to it.

The superbly ironic introduction is so artfully composed as to be obviously ironic only when reviewed in the light of what follows. The nineteenth-century editor Dean Milman put it beautifully when he wrote, "Divest this whole passage of the latent sarcasm betrayed by the subsequent tone of the whole disquisition, and it might commence a Christian history written in the most Christian spirit of candour." Armed with this warning, we may look in Gibbon's "candid but rational inquiry into the progress and establishment of Christianity" for the evidence that he enjoys the melancholy duty imposed upon the historian, who must "discover the inevitable mixture of error and corruption which [religion] contracted in a long residence upon earth, among a weak and degenerate race of beings."

Both the substance and the manner of the inquiry are well illustrated in the third paragraph of the fifteenth chapter:

Our curiosity is naturally prompted to inquire by what means the Christian faith obtained so remarkable a victory over the established religions of the earth. To this inquiry an obvious but satisfactory

answer may be returned; that it was owing to the convincing evidence
of the doctrine itself, and to the ruling providence of its great Author.
But as truth and reason seldom find so favourable a reception in the
world, and as the wisdom of Providence frequently condescends to use
the passions of the human heart, and the general circumstances of
mankind, as instruments to execute its purpose, we may still be
permitted, though with becoming submission, to ask, not indeed what
were the first, but what were the secondary causes of the rapid growth
of the Christian church?

The conditional, qualified sentences convey insidious doubts which
reflect back upon the seeming certainty of the obvious and satisfactory
answer to the first question. Indeed, the very fact that Gibbon disposes
so summarily of the first causes for the victory of Christianity makes us
doubt whether we ought to believe in either their sufficiency or their
actuality. We "may" return an orthodox answer to his first inquiry, but
a doubt has been insinuated into the inquiring mind by the summary
dismissal of the subject. Moreover, the reader is almost certain to attach
more importance to the secondary than to the primary causes of the
rise of Christianity, if the *History* dwells sufficiently long upon them.
Such is Gibbon's method in this chapter.
   The second part of the paragraph lists five secondary causes for the
rise of Christianity, and most of the remainder of this lengthy chapter is
concerned with their illustration and expansion. Gibbon's answer to his
own question—what were the secondary causes for the rise of
Christianity?—runs

It will, perhaps, appear that it was most effectually favoured and
assisted by the five following causes: I. The inflexible, and, if we may
use the expression, the intolerant zeal of the Christians, derived, it is
true, from the Jewish religion, but purified from the narrow and
unsocial spirit which, instead of inviting, had deterred the Gentiles from
embracing the law of Moses. II. The doctrine of a future life, improved
by every additional circumstance which could give weight and efficacy
to that important truth. III. The miraculous powers ascribed to the
primitive church. IV. The pure and austere morals of the Christians. V.
The union and discipline of the Christian republic, which gradually
formed an independent and increasing state in the heart of the Roman
empire.

Since the effect of the chapter lies in the way in which Gibbon writes
of each of these causes, we must now examine his treatment of each.

The first cause, Christian zeal, is traced from the peculiar rites, sullen obstinacy, and unsocial manners of the Jews, which are lightly contrasted with "the elegant mythology of the Greeks" and the tolerance of "the polite Augustus." Gibbon disregards any evidence of humanity or hints of Christian doctrine which may be contained in the Old Testament, and he arraigns the Jews for their disregard of gentlemanly manners and their ignorance of polite philosophy. Jewish fervor is represented as being equally irrational and inhumane: "The current of zeal and devotion, as it was contracted into a narrow channel, ran with the strength and sometimes with the fury of a torrent." The image of the raging water is a good example of the way in which Gibbon succeeds in insinuating ridicule—had their zeal only run with the strength of a torrent, the idea would have commanded respect; when the word fury is added it evokes, as it is meant to do, a sardonic twitch of the lip. He is more directly ironical when he tells us that the Jews "had been commanded to extirpate some of the more idolatrous tribes, and the execution of the divine will had seldom been retarded by the weakness of humanity." The real annoyance which Gibbon feels has its roots in the Jewish lack of common sense. Their reverence for the miracles of the Old Testament receives short shrift in the remark that "that singular people seems to have yielded a stronger and more ready assent to the traditions of their ancestors than to the evidence of their own senses."

The Christians are said to have adopted all the least attractive vices of the Jews and even to have added a few of their own. A footnote of the supposed cupidity of the Christians smears them with one of the failings traditionally ascribed to the Jews: "Even the reverses of the Greek and Roman coins were frequently of an idolatrous nature. Here indeed the scruples of the Christian were superseded by a stronger passion." There is a more general and more carefully calculated innuendo in his remarks upon the difficulties encountered by Christian commentators when they try to explain why the apostles observed Jewish rites and ceremonies while their successors do not: "the industry of our learned divines had abundantly (rather than adequately) explained the ambiguous language of the Old Testament and the ambiguous conduct of the apostolic teachers." The use of the alternative term "adequately" shows Gibbon's real meaning: that modern theologians are frauds. The repetition of "ambiguous" only darkens the smear over Jews and Christians alike. His enjoyment of irreverent comedy is revealed in his humorously alliterative remarks upon the Gnostics who "Averse to the pleasures of sense . . . morosely arraigned the polygamy of the Patriarchs, the gallantries of David, and the seraglio of Solomon."

It is as much the style as the substance of the paragraphs from which the above examples are taken which may persuade the reader to share the historian's dislike of Jewish customs and his scorn for early Christian dissensions. Sectarian disputes are too closely analogous to those of the English Civil War for Gibbon to be able to write dispassionately about them. We should not lose sight of the fact that Gibbon's own feelings about the importance of rationality induce him to be scathing about the feelings of others. It is through irony and innuendo that zeal, the first cause for the success of Christianity, is shown to be discreditable.

A similar rational skepticism disposes quietly but firmly of the second cause: the doctrine of the immortality of the soul. Gibbon's main attack is directed by the sort of mechanico-materialism which goes back as far at least as Hobbes. The historian says coldly, "A doctrine thus removed beyond the senses and the experience of mankind might serve to amuse the leisure of a philosophic mind . . . [but it] . . . was rejected with contempt by every man of a liberal education and understanding." To reject the doctrine of the immortality of the soul with similar frigidity we only need to share Gibbon's conviction that rational proof and sensory evidence are synonymous, and incontrovertible. It is the fact of this conviction which transforms Gibbon's Christian apologetics and his explanation of Christian doctrine into sneers; as when he affirms that "there is nothing, except a divine revelation, that can ascertain the existence" of a future state; or concludes with apparent blandness his explanation that the Jews had not believed in the immortality of the soul with the statement that it was therefore "still necessary that the doctrine of life and immortality, which had been dictated by nature, approved by reason, and received by superstition, should obtain the sanction of divine truth from the authority and example of Christ." The inference that divine truth and superstition are frequently one must surely be drawn from this sentence; and, if it is drawn, then there is nothing for it but to admire the logic of the celebrated sneer about "so advantageous an offer" as eternal happiness being made to Christians "on condition of adopting the faith, and of observing the precepts of the Gospel." The reader is expected to draw the rational conclusion from such evidence—that zeal, superstition, intolerance, and fear contributed to the spread of the doctrine of the existence and immortality of the soul.

When Gibbon comes to the third cause, he is able to express his doubts freely since he knows that they are shared even by contemporary theologians. The substance of his attack upon the reality of miracles is contained in a careful antithesis: "every friend to revelation is persuaded of the reality, and every reasonable man is convinced of the cessation of miraculous powers." We know that all friends to revelation are to be classified as zealots whose enthusiasms are delusive. Only the superstitious can believe that God would suspend the laws of nature: they are, after all, His own laws; and it would be foolish to imagine Him repenting of them—even for the service of religion. Gibbon pursues the logic of his argument by extending it to "the authentic wonders of the evangelic history." He does not risk legal prosecution by saying that he doubts the truth of the miracles recorded in the Gospels. Instead, he affirms, with a specious air of impartial candor, that these wonders may be believed with far greater justice than the later miracles; but it is clear that he expects the reader to believe in neither.

When the reader comes to the fourth cause, the pure and austere morals of the Christians, he is confronted with what Dean Milman fairly called the most uncandid paragraphs in the *History*. Gibbon's arguments against asceticism are used to ridicule the practice of chastity, temperance, economy, and all the sober and domestic virtues. He makes it a source of reproach to his devout predecessors that they disdained, or affected to disdain, every earthly or corporeal delight; and he implies at the same time that they were hypocritical in merely pretending to this purity. His arguments against asceticism and his air of stoic superiority to Christian virtue are amusing rather than convincing, and the humor is touched with salaciousness. While he admits that the bishops at least were celibate and chaste, Gibbon comments disingenuously that the "loss of sensual pleasure was supplied and compensated by spiritual pride." Later in the *History* this renunciation of earthly marriage and of family ties is said to be more than made up for by the bishops' "faculty of spiritual generation"—their power of consecrating and thus multiplying their spiritual progeny, the priests.

The fifth cause for the rise of Christianity—the growth of a Christian state within the secular state—is the one upon which Gibbon dwells the longest. Again he acknowledges the practical good sense which underlies the forms of church government as they gradually developed, and again he manages to imply that the organization and concentration of power in the hands of bishops demonstrated a discreditable degree of worldliness among the Christians. Of synods, or local church councils, he says that "the institution was so well suited to private ambition and to public interest, that in the space of a few years it was received throughout the whole empire"; and he connects the establishment of an ecclesiastical hierarchy with the increasing intolerance of the church. By means of a constant flow of inferences of this kind, Gibbon demonstrates, to his own satisfaction, the all-too-human nature of those who attempted or pretended to establish divine institutions upon earth. He finds in them a mixture of pride, greed, avarice, and thwarted impulse which discredits the institution which they built; and he establishes a point of view hostile to doctrinal Christianity and to the church as a human invention without ever making a direct statement which might have been legally actionable. Humanists of the eighteenth century had learned to disguise their doubts beneath a thin cloak of irony.

This irony is implicit in Gibbon's curt summary of the five causes which he had discredited as "exclusive zeal, the immediate expectation of another world, the claim of miracles, the practice of rigid virtue, and the constitution of the primitive church." The tone of the summary makes it impossible for the reasonable man to sympathize with the first four causes because the language conveys both doubt and ridicule. We may easily suppose that the early Christians had little time for cultivating the finer arts of civilization—for those activities which, Gibbon tells us, may exercise the leisure of a liberal mind—namely, the acquisition of knowledge, the exercise of our reason or fancy, and the cheerful flow of unguarded conversation. He insists that the love of pleasure—even of intellectual pleasure—would have been abhorrent to the early Fathers, and he points out that their asceticism necessarily excluded them from polite society.

In contrast with this foolish Christian faith, the realistic skepticism of the pagan Romans is admirably attuned to the reason of the eighteenth century. The Romans, he notes, had not really believed in any of the pagan religions: "On public occasions the philosophic part of mankind affected to treat with respect and decency the religious institutions of their country, but their secret contempt penetrated through the thin and awkward disguise." This sentence surely reveals the attitude of the historian to the official creed and lax practice of the established church of his own day. As we read on, we may understand why the pious were shocked by him; and we may see where his skepticism penetrated through the thin and elegant disguise of his style. If we were to omit the careful qualifications introduced into his paragraph upon the success of superstition, we should be able to cull from it the following seemingly dispassionate assertions:

the practice of superstition is so congenial to the multitude that, if they are forcibly awakened, they still regret the loss of their pleasing vision. . . . So urgent upon the vulgar is the necessity of believing, that the fall of any system of mythology will most probably be succeeded by the introduction of some other form of superstition. . . . Those who are inclined to pursue this reflection, instead of viewing with astonishment the progress of Christianity, will perhaps be surprised that its success was not still more rapid and still more universal.

In fact, these statements are separated from one another by several sentences of disarming qualification which make more graceful and indirect two insinuations: that Christianity is a superstition with a mythology, and that eighteenth-century Christianity is as much a superstition as were other religions of the past.

In the last few paragraphs of the chapter, the author virtually identifies himself with the pagan scoffers whose opinions of Christianity he records; he establishes the following inferences as if they were facts: that the first Christians were mean and ignorant; that learned and wealthy Christians were few; that Christianity was most favorably received by the poor and simple; and that the educated pagans, considering the Christians only as obstinate and perverse enthusiasts, overlooked the fulfillment of prophecy and the working of miracles which were going on around them. The first three inferences might be damaging to the intellectual respectability of Christianity, but the last one really strikes the hardest blow at the miraculous foundations of the Christian religion.

Gibbon asks, in his last paragraph, "how shall we excuse the supine inattention of the Pagan and philosophic world to those evidences which were presented by the hand of Omnipotence, not to their reasons, but to their senses?" In a lengthy answer to his own rhetorical question, he reveals that there are no pagan records of the Christian miracles, nor of the great natural phenomenon recorded in the New Testament—the great darkness which fell upon the earth at the crucifixion. The inference which the reader is expected to draw is perfectly clear, and it completes the historian's case: none of these things ever happened. This conclusion is the natural one for a triumphant rationalism.

After the rhetorical coruscations of Chapter XV, the more sober narration of Chapter XVI may seem something of an anticlimax; but Gibbon's account of the martyrdoms of the early Christians has a double purpose: the one is to show that the Christians exaggerated the number and sufferings of the martyrs; the other is to show that persecution of Christians by Christians has been as widespread and reprehensible as any pagan persecution. Gibbon's first task is to inculcate in the reader a sense of the unreasonableness of the early Christians in the face of what he chooses to describe as Roman toleration.

He admits initially "the deaths of a few eminent martyrs" and "a few authentic . . . facts" about the persecutions, and then he nullifies the effects of the admissions by two of his usual methods: he attacks the undoubted fictions put out in the early accounts, and he deliberately belittles the instances of heroism which he reluctantly records. Although he admits the exalted merit of the real martyrs, he maintains that there were very few of them; and he also appears to believe that the Roman magistrates (who had been accused by Christian apologists of vindictive persecution) did in fact behave like educated eighteenth-century gentlemen—like men of polished manners and liberal education. Amongst the Romans, he says, "It was esteemed the duty of a humane judge to endeavour to reclaim rather than to punish, those deluded enthusiasts." We cannot wonder that an early nineteenth-century critic, Sir James Mackintosh, considered this chapter "a very ingenious and specious, but very disgraceful extenuation of the cruelties perpetrated by the Roman magistrates against the Christians." On the other hand, it is proper to recognize that Gibbon has related his facts correctly, even though he has, in Bury's words, "allowed his temperament to colour his history."

Gibbon's zealous distrust of zeal makes him blame the Christians for inviting persecution upon themselves. Indeed, he takes up for a moment one of the themes of the previous chapter when he attributes the misguided zeal and exclusiveness of the Christians to their Jewish inheritance, but he cannot find for the Christians any such excuse as he allows to the Jews for their illiberality, namely, the continuance of a long tradition and the sense of solidarity communicated by a national worship. Gibbon is probably correct in supposing that the rights of religious toleration within the Empire were held by mutual indulgence and that the intolerance of the proselytizing Christians was the real reason for persecution of them. When he tells us that the wild enthusiasm and airy speculations of the new sectaries caused every

Christian to prefer his private sentiment to the national religion, we may suspect that his fear of civil conflict lies behind the statement: good sense or reasonableness is our one sure defense against excesses.

In a spirit of such reasonableness, Gibbon now makes four statements about the Roman persecutions of the Christians for which he offers evidence in the body of the chapter. From his own attribution to the Romans of a quite eighteenth-century humanity and temperance, he draws four conclusions: "I. That a considerable time elapsed before they considered the new sectaries as an object deserving of the attention of government. II. That in the conviction of any of their subjects who were accused of so very singular a crime, they proceeded with caution and reluctance. III. That they were moderate in the use of punishments; and IV. That the afflicted church enjoyed many intervals of peace and tranquility." Modern research gives support to these conclusions, but it is not necessarily in sympathy with Gibbon's coloring of his narration, which is pleasantly dotted with ironic highlights.

His first ally in the substantiation of these statements is reason: "The total disregard of truth and probability in the representation of these primitive martyrdoms" enables him to dismiss the accounts of the early Fathers. The one martyr of some distinction, whose heroism Gibbon admits, is Cyprian. He goes to his death after he has partaken of an elegant supper in the company of his friends and after he had enjoyed all temporal consideration at the hands of the Roman authorities, and we are supposed to believe that the politeness of his persecutors makes such a death desirable. Some of Gibbon's suggestions are blandly scandalous—as when he tells us that "Marcia, the most favoured of [Commodus's] concubines, and who at length contrived the murder of her imperial lover, entertained a singular affection for the oppressed church." By the measured care of his style, Gibbon virtually removes the possibility that the reader should feel indignation or pity for the fates of the few martyrs whom he mentions. By the polish of his manner, the persecutions which took place under Pliny are made to appear mild, rational, and almost a source of pleasure to the victims. When, finally, he estimates the number of persons martyred under Diocletian, his amusement culminates in an urbane sarcasm reminiscent of, and perhaps borrowed from, Swift's *Modest Proposal*: he arrives at a total which "will allow an annual consumption of one hundred and fifty martyrs."

This tone most clearly reveals the scorn of the narrator for all forms of enthusiasm—and a special hostility to the zeal of the Christians.

(Perhaps, in Gibbon's view, a more rational Christianity would have invited quite different treatment.) But the most dangerously outspoken paragraph of the chapter is the one which describes—under color of transmitting educated Roman opinion—the life and purpose of Jesus Christ. If Gibbon's admiration of his humanity and of his human virtues is clear, his scorn for a doctrine founded upon revelation is even clearer in the daring application of the word "equivocal" to the circumstances of the Saviour's birth.

From this account of the notorious chapters, it can be seen that the so-called attack upon Christianity is really an attack upon the unmeasured enthusiasm of the Christians from the viewpoint of a rational skeptic who can yet subscribe to the ethical tenets of his national church: the excesses of the Zoroastrians and of the Mahometans receive the same coolly, and even comically, impartial treatment as the excesses of the Christians and of their partisan historians. Gibbon's attacks upon the effects of zeal in general (rather than upon the effects of particular doctrines) brings the first of the original quarto volumes to a close. He has reached a climax which has point and purpose within the plan of the whole *History*, and to this larger plan we must now return.

III   *The Christianity of Constantine*

Gibbon feared that the public of his own day had found the next installments of his *History*, the second and third volumes, more prolix and less entertaining than the first. Nearly two years elapsed between the publication of the first and the commencement of his second volume, and he found it so difficult to fulfill the promise made in the fourteenth chapter of the first volume—to relate the various transactions of the age of Constantine with order and clarity—that he destroyed his first draft. He was so successful in his second attempt that, in reading it, we can only be surprised at his misgivings.

The second volume of the *History* is not only entertaining but also beautifully ordered: it falls into two similarly arranged and parallel halves of five chapters each. The main subject of the first half is the lengthy reign of Constantine, with an account of his conversion to Christianity and its effects upon the religious and political life of the Empire; the second half gives almost equal space to the brief triumphs of Julian, his attempted restoration of paganism, and the Gothic incursions which follow his death. There is a continual awareness of the contrast between the dangers of Constantine's success and the glories of

Julian's failure, which seems designed to show the Christian emperor in
an unfavorable and the pagan emperor in a favorable light. Constantine's military pacification and long reign produce religious dissension; Julian's success in war is too brief to bring lasting peace to the
Empire. Though Gibbon is far too great a historian to tamper with the
facts at his disposal, the form of the volume insists that we make
comparisons between the thirty years of Constantine and the three
years of Julian as though their reigns were of similar importance to the
Empire. But this adjustment of scale does not prevent careful and
ample treatment of lesser emperors.

The opening paragraph of the seventeenth chapter and the second
volume resumes the main narrative after the digression on Christianity:

The unfortunate Licinius was the last rival who opposed the greatness,
and the last captive who adorned the triumph, of Constantine. After a
tranquil and prosperous reign the conqueror bequeathed to his family
the inheritance of the Roman empire; a new capital, a new policy, and a
new religion; and the innovations which he established have been
embraced and consecrated by succeeding generations. The age of the
great Constantine and his sons is filled with important events; but the
historian must be oppressed by their number and variety, unless he
diligently separates from each other the scenes which are connected
only by the order of time. He will describe the political institutions that
gave strength and stability to the empire before he proceeds to relate
the wars and revolutions which hastened its decline. He will adopt the
division unknown to the ancients of civil and ecclesiastical affairs: the
victory of the Christians, and their intestine discord, will supply
copious and distinct materials both for edification and for scandal.

The pleasure which the author takes in his own pretty triplet "a new
capital, a new policy, and a new religion" is evident; and his careful
equation of descriptive nouns—"edification" with "civil affairs" and
"scandal" with "ecclesiastical"—is surely intentional: these devices
establish the tone of the resumed political history.

This first of the three chapters about the civil and military
government of Constantine and his immediate successors consists
largely of a factual description of three important matters: the
establishment of the city of Constantinople as the new capital of the
Empire; the growth of a new, more elaborate hierarchy of government;
and the system of taxation by which the stability of the Empire was
maintained. What is most striking about the description is the note of
warning which it repeatedly strikes in the midst of Constantine's
prosperity, reminding us that in the very greatness of the Empire lie the

seeds of its own decay. Even at this early stage of the *History* Gibbon has it clearly in mind that the decline of the Empire begins with the translation of the capital from West to East.

In one of Gibbon's lengthiest passages of description, decorated by frequent Classical allusions, he outlines, in tones of almost enthusiastic admiration, the historical and geographical situation of Byzantium which has supplanted Rome. But respect for the emperor's success is tempered by amusement at his vanity and superstition: "The prospect of beauty, of safety, and of wealth, united in a single spot" is said to be sufficient to justify Constantine's choice; but we are also told that he attributed the choice of site to the inspiration of a heavenly vision. The rapidity of the city's construction is attributed to the impatient vanity of the emperor, and the ultimate fall of the capital is prognosticated in the warning that Constantine compensates his citizens for civil and religious slavery by granting them the fatal and luxurious ease which had already brought about the decline of ancient Rome.

In describing the new hierarchy of government, Gibbon spares no pains to emphasize the Oriental ostentation and the proliferation of titles and offices, each with its train of new and servile dependents. The army itself is weakened by the admission of barbarians, who have to be enlisted because the Romans now fear the military service in which they had glorified in the days of republican freedom. Finally, the system of taxation which supported this already rickety edifice is made to appear crippling. We cannot do better than record the whole process in our author's own words:

When they lost even the semblance of those virtues which were derived from their ancient freedom, the simplicity of Roman manners was insensibly corrupted by the stately affectation of the courts of Asia. . . . As the sense of liberty became less exquisite, the advantages of order were more clearly understood. . . . As the spirit of jealousy and ostentation prevailed in the councils of the emperors, they proceeded with anxious diligence to divide the substance and to multiply the titles of power. . . . The divided administration, which had been formed by Constantine, relaxed the vigour of the state, while it secured the tranquillity of the monarch.

Can we fail to draw the conclusion that the true beginning of the decline and fall of the Empire is to be found during the reign of Constantine?

The next two chapters amply confirm this conclusion, for they relate the long list of unnatural murders which pollute the honor of the house of Constantine until the accession of Julian. Constantine is shown to degenerate morally in his later years and to murder his own sons on suspicion of their possible treason. In the course of Chapter XVIII, Crispus, Constantine II, and Constans are murdered or fall in battle, leaving Constantius as the sole surviving son to inherit the Empire at the end of the chapter. The gloom is a little lightened by an account of the virtues of the first Constantine; by the comedy of the paragraphs upon the premature coronation of Sapor, the unborn king of Persia; by the vivid description of Constantius's campaign in Persia; by the exciting narration of battles and conspiracies, interlaced with accounts of Sarmatian manners; and by a vivid picture of the catastrophic battle of Mursa which decimated the armies of Constantius and Magnentius, the two contenders for the imperial title, and weakened the Empire. Gibbon's style in this chapter varies from lofty panegyric to salacious comedy, from measured description to swift and violent action. All is made to display the pernicious tendency of the system introduced by Constantine, and we can only expect the gloom to deepen in the next chapter.

So well, however, does Gibbon marshal his materials, that the nineteenth chapter presents something very like a mirror image of its predecessor: there is a delightful, unexpected reversal of fortune when the virtuous, able Julian succeeds to the throne of his uncle and cousins. His tender regard for the peace and happiness of his subjects forms a marked and deliberate contrast with the luxurious autocracy of Constantius and with the brief tyranny of Julian's half-brother Gallus. The chapter ends with such solemn praise of Julian that we recognize him for the important character which he proves to be in the *History*, even while Gibbon turns from him for two chapters to write about the circumstances and the effects of Constantine's conversion to the Christian religion. The twentieth chapter suggests that this conversion was the real reason for the decline which has been described in the previous chapters.

In this chapter about Christianity, Gibbon employs the method used with such success in the fifteenth chapter: first, he admits the historical importance of the conversion; second, he asserts his own impartiality as historian; and, third, he proceeds to demonstrate the dubious spiritual value of the conversion and the certain material splendor resulting from it. In phrase after phrase from this chapter, we may feel Gibbon's skepticism about the emperor's sincerity: we may feel it in the statement of the spiritual advantages which Constantine might have expected to derive from deferring his baptism until his deathbed and also in the innuendo of the statement that "the liberality of Constantine increased in a just proportion to his faith and his vices." Gibbon indicates the comic nature of the emperor's inconsistencies when he declares that Constantine "artfully balanced the hopes and fears of his subjects, by publishing in the same year two edicts; the first of which enjoined the solemn observance of Sunday, and the second directed the regular consultation of the Aruspices," or when he tells us that the Christian emperor's filial piety "increased the council of Olympus by the solemn apotheosis of his father Constantius."

The attack is as amusing as it is artful, and it is almost impossible not to share Gibbon's attitude as we read. While he can admire the use and beauty of the Christian religion, he has nothing but scorn for some of the methods by which it was propagated. His commentary upon the emperor's supposed vision is in the best tradition of rational skepticism:

The protestant and philosophic readers of the present age will incline to believe that, in the account of his own conversion, Constantine attested a wilful falsehood by a solemn and deliberate perjury. They may not hesitate to pronounce that, in the choice of a religion, his mind was determined only by a sense of interest; and that (according to the expression of a profane poet) he used the altars of the church as a convenient footstool to the throne of the empire. A conclusion so harsh and so absolute is not, however, warranted by our knowledge of human nature, of Constantine, or of Christianity. In an age of religious fervour the most artful statesmen are observed to feel some part of the enthusiasm which they inspire; and the most orthodox saints assume the dangerous privilege of defending the cause of truth by the arms of deceit and falsehood. Personal interest is often the standard of our belief, as well as of our practice; and the same motives of temporal advantage which might influence the public conduct and professions of Constantine would insensibly dispose his mind to embrace a religion so propitious to his fame and fortunes.

Such a passage shows Gibbon and his century at their best in dealing with what they cannot understand and with what, therefore, they cannot appreciate. He is torn between admiration and annoyance: he wishes to admire the emperor as a rational man, and he can only do so at the price of turning him into a conscious hypocrite.

Gibbon deplores the division of power in the Roman state which was brought about by the spread of the Christian church, and he points out

the way in which the bishops increased their temporal power and
influence by setting up ecclesiastical courts separate from the civil
courts; by use of the religious sentences up to the final sanction of
excommunication; by preaching submission to the church; and by
gradually establishing the right to lay down a body of law for the
regulation of the church at the great church synods or councils. The last
sentence of this chapter reads: "The progress of time and superstition
erased the memory of the weakness, the passion, the ignorance which
disgraced these ecclesiastical synods; and the catholic world has
unanimously submitted to the *infallible* decrees of the general
councils." In other words, the church has been another agency in the
undermining of republican independence and virtue; and we may be led
to believe that this was a consequence of the impurity of the churches'
chief benefactor; for we have already seen that "the liberality of
Constantine increased in a just proportion to his faith and to his vices."
This impression is sedulously inculcated into, and successfully left
upon, the mind by Chapter XX as a suitable introduction to the schisms
and persecutions within the early church.

"The grateful applause of the clergy has consecrated the memory of
a prince who indulged their passions and promoted their interest.
Constantine gave them security, wealth, honours and revenge." Such is
the opening of the twenty-first chapter, a chapter in which Christian
precept is constantly confounded by Christian practice and in which
the passions of its ministers are shown to have disgraced and retarded
the progress of the newly established church. The place of honor in this
chapter is reserved to Athanasius, who becomes its central figure and is
almost the hero of a long series of doctrinal controversies. Gibbon's
partiality to him is confirmed by a footnote in the last volume which
tells us that the portrait of Athanasius was one of the passages of the
History with which the author was least dissatisfied. A modern reader
can hardly fail to admire the skill with which, having broken the
chronological thread of the narrative in order to relate this hero's
history from its beginning before the reign of Constantine, Gibbon
gradually leads back through the reign of Constantine to the general
history of Christianity within the Empire as it is illustrated in the
exciting incidents of the hero's life. The chapter is every bit as varied as,
and very much more exciting than, many an eighteenth-century novel.

This humane admiration of personal virtue and manly strength
prepares us to accept more readily the truth of the concluding
sentences of the chapter, that "The simple narrative of the intestine

divisions which distracted the peace, and dishonoured the triumph, of the church, will confirm the remark of a Pagan historian, and justify the complaint of a venerable bishop. The experience of Ammianus had convinced him that the enmity of the Christians towards each other surpassed the fury of savage beasts against man; and Gregory Nazianzen most pathetically laments that the kingdom of heaven was converted by discord into the image of chaos, of a nocturnal tempest, and of hell itself."

Gibbon underlines the lesson taught by such religious fanaticism when he points out that the metaphysical opinions of the sectaries had no influence upon their moral characters and that the practical results of religious controversies were almost wholly bad. The last paragraphs of the chapter complete the first half of the volume by summing up the triumphs of Christianity under Constantine and his sons. The second half of the volume shows the brief revival of paganism under Julian.

IV   *The Paganism of Julian*

In the second half of the second volume, the rise of a Christian emperor, Julian, who was subsequently converted to paganism, presents an interesting counterpart to the rise of a pagan emperor, Constantine, who was eventually converted to Christianity; and the fact that Gibbon gives almost equal space to the two reigns, although that of Julian was by far the shorter, implies that the historian attached equal importance to the two series of events and to the two emperors. In the twenty-second chapter, Julian is praised for the effectiveness of his active virtues; but, in the seventeenth chapter, which opens the volume and describes the administration of Constantine, the earlier emperor is accused of chicanery in the foundation of his new capital. Chapter XXII is distinguished by its note of sustained, temperate, and justified eulogy; for nowhere in the *History* does any other character appear to meet with as much favor as Julian or to bear so gracefully the weight of his author's approval. It is curious to reflect that Julian is particularly praised for the possession of qualities—humanity, self-sacrifice, and stoical endurance—for which, in another part of the *History*, Gibbon is constrained to admire a very different hero—Jesus Christ.

The feats which justify such praise are narrated swiftly and compellingly. By a brief reference back to the military victories of Julian in Gaul until the year 359, and to his restoration of law and order under an effective and upright administration, Gibbon reminds us of the pleasant anticipations of future prosperity which he had given at the end of Chapter XIX. Chapter XXII starts in the year 360, when the acclamations of Julian's devoted troops turn him into an emperor against his own wishes and compel him to defend his new dignity against the anger of Constantius. There is no more exciting or rapid piece of writing in the whole *History* than the passage in which Julian organizes his legions to defend his new title and himself marches, with a third of his forces, from the Rhine to Illyricum:

For himself Julian had reserved a more difficult and extraordinary part. He selected three thousand brave and active volunteers, resolved, like their leader, to cast behind them every hope of a retreat; at the head of this faithful band, he fearlessly plunged into the recesses of the Marcian, or Black Forest, which conceals the sources of the Danube; and, for many days, the fate of Julian was unknown to the world. The secrecy of his march, his diligence, and vigour, surmounted every obstacle; he forced his way over mountains and morasses, occupied the bridges or swam the rivers, pursued his direct course without reflecting whether he traversed the territory of the Romans or of the barbarians, and at length emerged, between Ratisbon and Vienna, at the place where he designed to embark his troops on the Danube. By a well-concerted stratagem he seized a fleet of light brigantines as it lay at anchor; secured a supply of coarse provisions sufficient to satisfy the indelicate, but voracious, appetite of a Gallic army; and boldly committed himself to the stream of the Danube. The labours of his mariners, who plied their oars with incessant diligence, and the steady continuance of a favourable wind, carried his fleet above seven hundred miles in eleven days; and he had already disembarked his troops at Bononia, only nineteen miles from Sirmium, before his enemies could receive any certain intelligence that he had left the banks of the Rhine.

The successes due to Julian's courage, resolution, endurance, and intelligence occupy almost two thirds of the chapter, before the sudden and premature death of Constantius—who was marching from Persia through Asia Minor to meet and to oppose him—made him sole emperor without further bloodshed. The last part of the chapter shows a Julian who refuses to add to the taxes of the Empire by maintaining the swarms of haughty menials which had swelled the Oriental pomp of Constantine and his sons. In a series of anecdotes, the contrast between his predecessors' corruption and his own simplicity is elegantly and forcibly depicted. The thousand barbers, the thousand cupbearers, the thousand cooks, and the swarms of eunuchs were dismissed; and, by a single edict, Julian reduced the palace of Constantinople to an immense desert. The corrupt were punished, the law was rigidly upheld, and the example of the emperor animated the virtues of his subjects. If we can believe his eulogist

In one and the same day he gave audience to several ambassadors, and wrote or dictated a great number of letters to his generals, his civil magistrates, his private friends, and the different cities of his dominions. He listened to the memorials which had been received, considered the subject of the petitions, and signified his intentions more rapidly than they could be taken in short-hand by the diligence of his secretaries. He possessed such flexibility of thought, and such firmness of attention, that he could employ his hand to write, his ear to listen, and his voice to dictate; and pursue at once three several trains of ideas without hesitation, and without error.

How much more active and effective are Julian's virtues made to seem than all the efforts of his predecessor, Constantine, in founding his new capital! On the one hand, we are shown a magnificent and luxury-loving Oriental despot; on the other, a ruler of great abilities, simple tastes, and stoic endurance. In one respect only are the two emperors delightfully and ludicrously similar: they are both subject, or profess to be subject, to the influence of visions.

While the contrast between the two men and the two reigns is a real one, supported by historical evidence, few modern historians would see it quite in Gibbon's terms; and it is useful to consider another point of view before we pass to Julian's treatment of Christianity. Constantine is pictured by a modern historian, G. P. Baker, as "a tall slender, dark man, with an aquiline nose and almost ascetic face of the kind frequently seen in British naval officers and in a familiar type of New Englander."[2] Julian, on his first appearance at the Eastern court, is said to have looked like "a wild backwoodsman, with the manners, and even the thoughts of a prehistoric age."[3] This same historian credits Constantine with a forward-looking mind, which could see the stability of the Empire in the establishment of an effective monarchy upon the principle of a hereditary succession, with an adequate civil service to support it and to administer justice according to law. According to him, Julian's measures all looked back to the days of the Antonines and of the republic; his reduction of the royal household was also a weakening of the structure of government; his abolition of espionage (the royal secret service) made him more vulnerable to conspiracy; and his religious revolution introduced a new source of confusion into the

Empire. It may well be that Julian showed his best qualities most successfully before he became emperor in his humane administration of Gaul according to the system of Constantine. He was personally agreeable, but he was not qualified to revive republican virtue or to replace it with an effective new system. His defects are shown in his attempts to destroy Christianity.

In view of the way in which the Christians are treated in earlier chapters, it might perhaps be expected that Gibbon would view with favor the attempts of Julian to restore paganism as the official religion of the Empire; but the historian is philosopher enough—and Christian enough—to decry all baseless superstition and to rejoice that even "the genius and power of Julian were unequal to ... restoring a religion which was destitute of theological principles, of moral precepts, and of ecclesiastical discipline." In consequence, the twenty-third chapter is nicely balanced between a reprobation of the careless, fanatical Christians who failed to bring up the future emperor with an intelligent appreciation of the truths of their religion, and an exposure of the barren claims of the philosophic pagans to unlock the mysteries of hidden wisdom or to reveal them by magic and miracle.

Julian had been reared as a Christian in Asia Minor, where the quarrels of his coreligionists and the arrogant claims of the various sectaries to have a monopoly of revealed truths disgusted him so much that, when his half-brother Gallus became emperor of the East and they were both freed from Christian tutelage, he used his liberty to experience what had previously been forbidden to him—the pleasures of polite literature and the practices of pagan religion. Whilst he continued for a long time to appear to be a Christian, he did in fact study Platonic doctrines with pagan philosophers, and he adopted with enthusiasm the worship of the pagan gods whose reality and power seemed to be proved in the miracles performed by such sophists as Maximus. Gibbon accuses the young man of a most unphilosophical credulity: the miracles performed by the sophists were mere magic and conjuring, but they convinced Julian, who was initiated into the Eleusinian mysteries in the year 351.

When Julian became emperor some ten years later, he established a universal toleration of all the religions practiced within the Empire; and the historian comments sardonically that the only hardship he inflicted on the Christians was "to deprive them of their power of tormenting their fellow-subjects, whom they stigmatised with the odious titles of idolators and heretics." From the first, his toleration was touched with malice towards the religion which he had abandoned, and Julian the Apostate (as the Christians called him) derived considerable intellectual amusement from the theological disputes of the hostile Christian sects whom he invited to pursue their discussions in his palace so that he might "enjoy the agreeable spectacle of their furious encounters." In such ways he fed his scorn for the faith in which he had, unwillingly, been reared.

His scheme of toleration included, however, the active encouragement of all non-Christian religions. The Jews were pressed to rebuild the Temple at Jerusalem and did, in fact, proceed with the restoration for some six months until repeated interventions of a miraculous nature, and the death of Julian, put an end to the attempt. Where Christian congregations had destroyed pagan temples and erected churches to purify the old foundations, the laws of Julian gave the original owners the right to demand a restitution, which involved both compensation for the ruin and the rebuilding of the temple on the site of the church. It is now the turn of the pagans to appear in the *History* as religious iconoclasts who destroy churches, torture their opponents singly, and massacre them collectively in the insanity of their enthusiasm.

By such anecdotes as that of the torture of Mark, bishop of Arethusa, Gibbon convinces us that it is not religion which is the object of his attack, but rather the debasement of human nature under the influence of religious zeal. The pagan magistrates inflicted upon Mark the torture with which Autolycus threatens the clown in *The Winter's Tale*: he was scourged, anointed with honey, and hung up in a net to endure the heat of the Syrian sun and the stings and bites of noxious insects. The aged bishop bore the trial with fortitude and survived to enjoy the honor of this triumph over his persecutors. Gibbon admires, pities, and respects him. Fortunately for the Empire, Julian died before the deadly spirit of fanaticism had entirely perverted his feelings, his mind, and his virtues, and had induced him to run the risk of starting a civil war in the attempt to restore the exclusive worship of the pagan gods.

In the next chapter, the twenty-fourth, the history of Julian's twenty-month reign is concluded in a lengthy description of the emperor's expedition into Asia to chastise the Persian emperor, Sapor. This enterprise, which began with every promise of success, was defeated by the desertion of his allies, by the skillful deception of the Persians, and by Julian's own death upon the field of battle. Gibbon makes it clear that vanity had been one of the motives of Julian's campaign, but the account of the advance into Assyria, of the sieges of Persabor and Maogamalcha, and of the crossing of the Tigris to win a battle at the very gates of the Persian capital, Ctesiphon, is almost as exciting as the description of the military operations by which Julian first won the Empire.

Outside Ctesiphon, however, Julian had to face the ever-increasing might of Persian reinforcements from the provinces and the frontiers; and he decided upon a retreat up the course of the Tigris through a hostile country which was burned and wasted like a desert before him. He was perpetually harassed by growing Persian armies and, at last, in a battle in the mountains, he was fatally wounded; and the victory gained by his enraged soldiers was made useless by his death. Gibbon transcribes from Ammianus the emperor's dying speech, a masterpiece of philosophic serenity and acceptance; and by so doing he induces us to admire the amiable inconsistency and transparent humanity of the dying Julian in bewailing the death of his friend Anatolius, who was killed in the same battle. Such was the end of the pagan whom Gibbon thought worthy of comparison with the great Constantine.

Julian is made to share with his predecessor some of the blame for the triumph of Christianity and for the calamities to the Empire which followed his death because, though he was the last of his royal house, he had refused to nominate a successor who would continue his policies. Upon his death, the army nominated Jovian to extricate them from their difficulties. "The feeble hand of Julian's Christian successor" concluded a humiliating peace with the emissaries of Sapor, and the hard-pressed Romans escaped complete destruction by rendering up long-held provinces and fortresses to their crafty enemies. The effects of Julian's reign were, after all, similar to those of the reign of Constantine. The attempt to restore paganism was a failure and contributed to the weakening of the Empire by the exacerbation of religious quarrels; the pursuit of military glory was disastrous, and Julian's failure precipitated the final division of the Empire which comes about in the next chapter; this division, in its turn, encouraged the barbarian invasions and the settlement of the Goths within the boundaries of the Empire.

The twenty-fifth chapter shows how Jovian's successor, Valentinian, was driven to divide the Empire with his brother Valens. Valentinian had very little difficulty with his Roman subjects in the West, but the first duty of Valens in the East was to put down the rebellion of

Procopius. Valentinian continued the universal religious toleration of his predecessors, but Valens allowed himself to appear as the protector of the Arian party in the Christian church.[4] For twelve years there was a truce between the religious factions, which helped to cool their tempers; and Gibbon forgives much of the personal intemperance of Valentinian because he did succeed in moderating the quarrels of the Christians and in regulating the rapacity of the clergy.

This modest success did not save either of the emperors from the constant necessity of prosecuting military operations to save their dominions from the effects of revolts from within and invasions from without their borders. Gibbon groups his accounts of these operations under the various territories in which they took place, and, in doing so, he expresses perhaps something of his sense of the disruption of the Empire. With the descriptions of wars, he recapitulates details of the social and economic histories of the various peoples whom he treats; and these prevent the chapter from being merely a narrative of similar crimes. The personal virtues of Valentinian, courage, simplicity, and valor, are insufficient to atone for his frequent savagery; to counter the weakness of his timorous brother Valens; or to mitigate the uneven administration of his lieutenants in war and peace. The division of the Empire between the two brothers is the outstanding historical fact of this chapter, and the evil effects of division are amply demonstrated. The last paragraphs of the chapter show how this division was productive of additional weakness in the succession upon their father's death of both the sons of Valentinian to the Western Empire. Gratian, the elder, actually ruled, although the government was carried on in the name of his four-year-old half-brother Valentinian II.

The twenty-sixth chapter which concludes the second volume leads to one single event which had permanent results in the weakening of the Empire: the crossing of the Danube by the Goths. This is a prelude to the general invasions of Goths, Huns, and Vandals which bring the Western Empire to an end in the third volume. Since the Goths were hard pressed by the Huns, Gibbon expounds the manners and history of the nomadic, pastoral nations to account for the disasters which end the reign of Valens. He points out that their carnivorous diet might make them more fierce, that the simplicity of their lives inured them to hardship, and that "the amusements of the chace serve as the prelude to the conquest of an empire." When the Huns were driven from China, they began to move west and eventually came into contact, and therefore into conflict, with the barbarian nations who had preceded them. Their first victims were the Goths, who had recently been defeated by Valens and his generals in three years of warfare which had persuaded them to stay on the north side of the Danube.

Only a year after Valens' victories, he allowed the Goths to seek refuge from the Huns on the Roman side of the Danube, under the pretense that the Gothic armies would now form the Empire's first line of defense. Within a few months, the Goths were in revolt against the imprudent slights and injustices which the Romans had inflicted upon them; and Valens found himself obliged to fight his newest allies. He refused to wait for the assistance of Gratian, who was marching to meet him with all the forces of the West; and he committed his own armies in the battle of Salices and the culminating disaster of Hadrianople. When Gratian, who had been hampered by a war in Gaul, at last arrived in the East, it was to find his uncle dead, the Goths plundering and burning the Eastern provinces, and two-thirds of the Eastern armies destroyed.

His first task was to find a new emperor for the East, and his choice fell upon Theodosius, who deserved all his colleague's confidence and began his reign with a three-year-long campaign which obtained a final capitulation of the Goths in the East. Gratian defeated the Ostrogoths in a similar campaign in the West in 386, and the defeated race was allowed once more to settle within the bounds of the Empire—in Thrace, in Phrygia, and in Lydia—on condition of providing an army of forty thousand for the defense of the Empire. As Gibbon weighs the results of this settlement, he warns us that its success will depend upon the ability of Theodosius to maintain peace between the rival factions among the Goths, but he foresees the eventual possibility that they might acquire the habits of industry and obedience; that their manners might be polished by time, education, and the influence of Christianity; and that they would eventually intermarry with the Romans and become Romans indeed. At the end of his second volume, the situations of both Eastern and Western Empires are precarious because of the presence of this enemy within.

To traverse, as briefly as we have done, the mighty maze of one of Gibbon's volumes is to see that it is not without a plan, and the plan is in essence simple: it is to demonstrate the sources and the progress of Roman weakness, and, in so doing, to demonstrate those weaknesses of universal human nature which are, in the end, self-destructive. If we look for villains in this volume, they are not so much particular Roman emperors, or particular tribes of barbarians, or groups of believers, Christian or pagan; the villains are ease, sloth, and luxury; enthusiasm, zeal, and fanaticism; arrogance, pride, and vanity. They are seen, as they must be, as embodied in particular persons, classes and races, philosophies and religions; but the real culprit is the uneducated, irrational, and (if we may use such an expression when writing of Gibbon's work) unregenerate human nature. It is the repeated consciousness that their lot may well be ours which gives enduring fascination to the lives of Romans and barbarians, Christians and pagans, emperors and plebeians.

Equally, in the lives of the great emperors, Constantine and Julian; or in the constancy of the saints, Athanasius and Mark of Arethusa; or in the nobility and stoicism of less well-known heroes like the first Theodosius and the Gothic leader, Fravitta, there is the possibility of man so controlling and ordering and directing his life as to demonstrate the highest of which he is capable; and Gibbon never withholds his own or his readers' admiration for the highest human achievements when they are to be found. If history is the record of the follies, vices, and crimes of mankind, there is still much to be learned from a lively representation of them; and Gibbon's consistent view of human nature is so persuasively presented in the antithetical portraits of Volume II as to make us share it. Though the Empire has yet some way to fall, the prospect of the third volume will not be one of unrelieved gloom so long as we are interested in human nature, and share the hope that it may be educated and refined into heroism and decency.

V   The Fall of the West

While the history contained in the third volume is naturally a continuation of the chronological narrative from the second, this volume shows as many signs as the previous one of a careful master plan and is in itself a complete artistic whole. The material of the volume is disposed with beautiful and unobtrusive symmetry around the main subject of the *History* and of the volume: the division of the Empire. The importance of this division is underlined by the construction of the volume in two halves (of six chapters each), which are mirror images of one another. At the center of the volume, a chapter on the Eastern Empire is mirrored by a companion chapter on the Western Empire. Two chapters describing Alaric the Goth and his sack of Rome precede the chapter on the Eastern Empire: their mirror image, following the chapter on the Western Empire, consists of two chapters on the successes of Attila the Hun. Gibbon completed the symmetry of the volume by balancing the three opening chapters which precede Alaric with a group of three concluding chapters to follow Attila; and he used this careful grouping to underline his themes and his sense of historical truth. For example, each group has at its center a religious chapter: the decline of paganism and rise of Christianity described in the one is ironically complemented by the success of monastic life and the start of barbarian persecutions portrayed in its fellow. Furthermore, while the third chapter of the volume records the division of the Empire under Arcadius and Honorius, its mirror image describes the final destruction of the Western Empire—almost as though the one event had led up to the other. The perfecting touch to the symmetry of the volume is provided by the complementary first and last chapters; for the secular and religious history of the declining Roman Empire with which the volume begins is paralleled with the establishment of the new Frankish civilization under the Christian convert, Clovis, with which it ends. This balance and order are made clearer in the following plan:

Chapters
XXVII   Secular and religious history to the death of Theodosius
XXVIII   Decline of paganism and rise of Christianity
XXIX   Division of Empire under Arcadius and Honorius
XXX, XXXI   Alaric
XXXII   Eastern Empire
XXXIII   Western Empire
XXXIV, XXXV   Attila
XXXVI   Sack of Rome by Genseric, total extinction of Western Empire
XXXVII   Monastic life and barbarian persecution
XXXVIII   Reign and conversion of Clovis

Although this plan is a gross oversimplification of the material of the chapters, it does suggest the orderliness of Gibbon's composition and his grasp of an enormous mass of historical materials within a clear pattern of his own making. If we can keep this pattern in mind while discussing the separate chapters, it will help us to feel the fundamental order and intention of the volume as it shows the similar weaknesses of East and West.

But the third volume does not exist in isolation from the total work. In order to emphasize the continuity of the whole narrative, Gibbon opens Chapter XXVII and his third volume with the death of Gratian, whose career played so important a part in the Roman assimilation of the Goths, described in the last two chapters of the second volume.

There is a mixture of civil with religious history in this chapter which reestablishes our sense of an intimate and sinister connection between the rise of the Christian religion and the fall of the Empire. However, the climax of the chapter is a cheerful one: the Empire is to be temporarily reunited under the virtuous Christian emperor, Theodosius.

The plan of the chapter is simple. The murder of the Western emperor, Gratian, leaves Theodosius powerless to take an immediate revenge upon the usurper, Maximus, with whom he therefore concludes a treaty of friendship, stipulating only that Maximus should remain beyond the Alps and leave Italy to the second Valentinian, who was still a minor. The middle of the chapter tells of the ruin of the Arian party in the Eastern church, and presents as companion pieces portraits of Ambrose, archbishop of Milan, and Theodosius, emperor of the East. The archiepiscopal vigor, courage, and ability are compared with the outstanding virtues and the regrettably hasty temper of the emperor. Then Theodosius is obliged to take up arms against Maximus for attempting to supplant Valentinian and, by defrauding him, restores Valentinian to the Western Empire. Valentinian is murdered by the usurping Arbogastes who, in his turn, is defeated; and the reunion of the two halves of the Empire under Theodosius completes a triumphant reign. But his premature death brings an end to the brief period of reunion and puts his two weak sons, Arcadius and Honorius, on the thrones of the two halves of the Empire in time for a new chapter.

In this chapter on Theodosius, the epigrammatic grasp of the subject matter and the power of insidious innuendo remain, but they are more discreetly used than they had been in, for instance, the coruscating twenty-first chapter. The narrative is speedy, showing all the historian's best qualities without excessive ornament, and never subordinating truth to entertainment. Its last paragraphs return with solemnity to the causes of the decline and fall: we are given an admonitory picture of the Romans who are fearfully enjoying what sensory pleasures still remain to them instead of affirming their manly virtue in the defense of the Empire; and we are shown how feeble the Roman infantry had become when, in the reign of Gratian, they were allowed to stop wearing armor because it was uncomfortably heavy.

Since Chapter XXVII concludes with this hint of disasters to befall the Empire under the sons of Theodosius, the words "Final Destruction" in the heading of the next chapter come as no surprise; but it is the final destruction of paganism to which they refer. By inserting this chapter of religious history between the successes of Theodosius and the failures of his sons, Gibbon again associates the success of Christianity with the weakening of the Empire. The chapter shows the Christian victory over pagan superstition to have been a Pyrrhic one, since many of the pagan practices were unconsciously assimilated into the Christian worship. Gibbon notes in particular that the faith was propagated with the help of a whole army of legendary martyrs; that there was a suspicious multiplication of miracles to authenticate the relics of long-buried saints; that the saints themselves came to be worshiped like the minor deities of the pagan religions; and that the ceremonies of the Christian churches adopted incense, perfumes, and artificial light to enhance their worship, as the pagan temples had done before them. His comment upon all this is made in a spirit of the calmest rationality: "The most respectable bishops had persuaded themselves that the ignorant rustics would more cheerfully renounce the superstitions of Paganism, if they found some resemblance, some compensation, in the bosom of Christianity. The religion of Constantine achieved, in less than a century, the final conquest of the Roman empire: but the victors themselves were insensibly subdued by the arts of their vanquished rivals." Unassisted human nature inevitably sinks to superstitious practices, and the vulgar Christians are no better (and no worse) in their foolish credulity than the pagans were before them.

The next chapter relates the story of the Empire under the divided rule of Arcadius and Honorius as though there were a causal connection between religious victory and military failure. The weakness of these two emperors is clearly shown in the fact that the chapter is as much concerned with the acts of their favorites and ministers, Rufinus and Stilicho, as with their own. Arcadius, in the East, had trusted Rufinus as his chief minister although Rufinus showed his extreme avarice and cruelty as soon as Theodosius was dead. Ultimately, Stilicho marched against him with the Western armies, on the pretense of offering help in a new Gothic war. But Stilicho's soldiers murdered Rufinus at a ceremonial review. Although Honorius was emperor for twenty-eight years, he was incapable of ruling and passed "the slumber of his life a captive in his palace, a stranger in his country, and the patient, almost the indifferent, spectator of the ruin of the Western empire. . . ." The division of the Empire has weakened it irremediably, and the separated halves appear to be in greater danger (because the emperors operated as rivals instead of as allies) than the top-heavy whole ever was.

The next two chapters relate the ruin of the Western Empire under the impact of Gothic invasions, the most important of which were led by Alaric, the epitome of the Gothic spirit. The invasions might better be described as rebellions, for the Goths involved in them were those who had been allowed to settle within the bounds of the Empire on the understanding that they would supply armies for its defense. In the first revolt, the dissatisfied Goths invaded the Illyrican and Greek provinces, and they were only stopped by the threatening advance of Stilicho from the West. The Goths' career of plunder and rapine was then rewarded by Arcadius, the emperor of the East, who seemed to fear the power and virtues of Stilicho more than the cruelties of Alaric. Alaric, instead of being punished for rebellion, was made master-general of Eastern Illyricum, where he was able to pursue his extortions legally with the full assent of Arcadius.

Alaric recruited his strength, and then advanced to attack the Western Empire. Stilicho repeatedly saved the West from Alaric's incursions and attacks, but the stupid Honorius allowed the wishes of a new favorite to procure the sudden disgrace and execution of Stilicho. The immediate consequence of such wicked folly was a new invasion of Italy by Alaric; with this event, Gibbon begins a new chapter. Following even worse advice, Honorius allowed his subjects to attack and pillage the families of his own Gothic armies, who were living as a sort of hostages for the soldiers' good behavior. Thirty thousand men deserted to the army of Alaric; and he, constantly frustrated by protracted negotiations, marched once more into the center of Italy and presented himself under the walls of Rome. Gibbon rightly insists upon the magnificence of this still immense and powerful city, upon the number of its inhabitants (which may have been as many as two million), upon their indolence and luxury, and upon their inability either to resist or to sustain a siege. Owing to Honorius's mismanagement, the city was three times besieged, thoroughly pillaged, and partially destroyed. Then Alaric left for the toe of Italy, pillaging every city that came in his way; and his progress was only stopped by his sudden death.

He was succeeded by a less sanguinary chieftain, Adolphus, who, as part of the price of a peace with Honorius, demanded and obtained the hand of the emperor's half-sister Placidia in marriage. Some of the Gothic spoils were returned to her by her husband as a magnificent marriage gift. She did not long enjoy her happiness, for her husband was murdered on a campaign to restore Spain to the allegiance of

Honorius; and, though *she* was eventually returned to her brother's court, the extreme parts of the Western Empire were lost in ruin. Britain declared its successful independence of the emperor, and Armorica (rather larger than the modern Brittany and Normandy) secured a more precarious independence. All Honorius could do, in an attempt to invigorate the government of the remainder of Gaul, was to institute an assembly of the seven remaining provinces. But the Gauls were so unused to independence and liberty that they did not know how to make use of them—either to restore the rule of law in public life or to defend themselves against their barbarian enemies. Their failure to use their freedom in either of these ways leads Gibbon to a conclusion often drawn in the *History*: "Under the mild and generous influence of liberty, the Roman empire might have remained invincible and immortal; or if its excessive magnitude, and the instability of human affairs, had opposed such perpetual continuance, its vital and constituent members might have separately preserved their vigour and independence."

The two central chapters of the volume now illustrate the evil effects of despotism and centralization; each series of disasters is ascribed to a failure of human virtue, which had been weakened by the practices of despotic government. The opening sentence of the chapter on the decay of the Eastern Empire makes a statement which Gibbon takes as an accepted truth and one which explains his treatment of the East in the remaining volumes of his *History*: "The division of the Roman world between the sons of Theodosius marks the final establishment of the empire of the East, which, from the reign of Arcadius to the taking of Constantinople by the Turks, subsisted one thousand and fifty-eight years in a state of premature and perpetual decay."

We may justly remark that it is a peculiar sort of decay which supports the existence of an empire for over a thousand years, and we may detect in the statement the weakness of a circular argument. Gibbon feels that passive obedience to an absolute monarch must enervate and degrade every faculty of the mind. Noting the establishment of such a monarchy, he concludes that the inhabitants of the Eastern Empire must, therefore, have been incapable of defending their lives and fortunes against the assaults of the barbarians or of defending their reason from the fear of superstition; and he proceeds to demonstrate that this was so. From this point, his interpretation of the events of the Eastern history is so affected by his dislike of superstition (in this case, of Christian superstition) as to make him write decline into every page, whereas the Eastern government was more effective than the tone of his commentary implies.

In Chapter XXXII we find that the inglorious reign of Arcadius at Constantinople—marked by the dominance, first, of the favorite Rufinus, and then of the eunuch Eutropius; disrupted by Gothic conspiracy and rebellion; and buffeted by religious disturbances centered upon the person of John Chrysostom—gave way to a long period during which the real power behind the throne was exercised by a woman, Pulcheria, the daughter of Arcadius and sister of Theodosius II. Perhaps the fact that she was a woman and a devout Christian prejudiced the historian unduly against her; for, while he admits her virtues, he appears to cast doubts upon their effectiveness. Yet her influence during the minority and reign of her incapable brother, Theodosius II, was to counteract his weaknesses and not only preserve intact the boundaries of his empire, but also extend them as the result of a Persian campaign.

A similar triumph of female rule was meanwhile attempted in the West. The thirty-third chapter provides an instructive parallel between East and West; Pulcheria is implicitly compared with Placidia. Placidia, half-sister to Honorius and widow of Adolphus the Goth, was married to Constantius, the successful general of Honorius, as a reward for his many victories, and he was also associated with Honorius in the government of the Western Empire. Constantius died in 421 after four years of marriage and seven months of imperial greatness, leaving his wife with a son, who became Valentinian III on the death of Honorius eighteen months later. Placidia had to seek temporary refuge with her children in the East; she obtained the help of her nephew, the Eastern Emperor Theodosius II, in establishing her son on the throne of the West and in investing her with the real power. Gibbon ascribes to her feminine weakness the success of the dark conspiracy of the general Aëtius against his rival, Boniface, who was governor of the African provinces. Such was the weakness of the government that the two generals decided their quarrel in a bloody battle, and the republic was deprived of the service of her two most illustrious champions while they were thus engaged in private strife.

Gibbon concludes this chapter of major disaster for the West with a pleasant exercise of his imagination in recounting the fable of the Seven Sleepers of Ephesus which he interprets as an allegorical representation of the astonishing changes which had taken place in the Empire in the course of the last two hundred years. No paraphrase can better the words of his own conclusion to the account:

. . . the seat of government had been transported from Rome to a new
seat on the banks of the Thracian Bosphorus; and the abuse of military
spirit had been suppressed by an artificial system of tame and
ceremonious servitude. The throne of the persecuting Decius was filled
by a succession of Christian and orthodox princes, who had extirpated
the fabulous gods of antiquity: and the public devotion of the age was
impatient to exalt the saints and martyrs of the catholic church on the
altars of Diana and Hercules. The union of the Roman empire was
dissolved; its genius was humbled in the dust; and armies of unknown
barbarians, issuing from the frozen regions of the North, had
established their victorious reign over the fairest provinces of Europe
and Africa.

But worse is to come: the next two chapters show Attila, king of the
Huns, to be an even more fearsome adversary of the remains of empire
than his awful predecessor, Alaric.

This thirty-fourth chapter has one of Gibbon's fascinating accounts
of the customs and habits of the barbarians (in this case, the Huns)
which often enliven his pages and show him to be a careful and exact
social historian. The embassy of Maximin to Attila, on behalf of
Theodosius, provides the opportunity for a description of barbarian
manners and of the temper of Attila, which occupies more of the
chapter than the horrifying descriptions of the previous desolation of
Eastern Europe by the Huns.

Attila only ceased to threaten the Eastern Empire when the death of
Theodosius II left Pulcheria sole empress in 450. She immediately
married Marcian, a senator of sixty, who was prepared to resist the
demands of Attila for additional sacrifices; when the barbarian again
threatened both the Eastern and Western Empires, the firmness of
Marcian contributed to persuade him to attack in the West. The
thirty-fifth chapter details the various successes of Attila in Gaul and in
Italy until he was finally defeated at Chalons.

After his death, the several barbarian kings who had been his allies
separated to seek their own individual fortunes; and there was some
hope that the courage and skill of the successful general Aëtius might
stave off for a long period the complete ruin of the West. Valentinian
III, who had long remained supine in indolence, took this moment to
raise his sword for the first time and to murder Aëtius, the one
remaining prop of his dubious empire, out of hatred and jealousy. Less

than a year later Valentinian was murdered in his turn. The day of Valentinian's murder, March 16, 455, seems to Gibbon to fulfill the ancient prediction that the Empire would last for twelve hundred years; for, if it could be said that Rome still survived, it did so with the loss of freedom, of virtue, and of honor. Attila, the barbarian Hun, and Valentinian, the indolent emperor, finally destroyed the West.

The last three chapters of the volume complete the story of the degeneration of the vast domains of the Western Empire into the brief circumference of a small barbarian kingdom in Italy; relate this decline to the rise and progress of monasticism; and, with an account of the reign of Clovis, suggest the beginnings of a new political and religious order which will develop into modern Europe. As the reign of Theodosius I had marked the last attempt to hold the old Empire together, so the reign of Clovis marks the beginning of a new European order; and the concluding chapters of the volume, which record the final destruction of old Rome, foreshadow the resurgence of the city as the seat of a religious leader, and actually show the limited success of the semi-Christianized barbarians who were better able to rule the old Empire than its original inhabitants.

The thirty-sixth chapter begins with yet another sack of Rome— this one by the Vandals, who, under Genseric, continued to ravage the Mediterranean coasts of the Empire, and who now signalized their real power to avenge themselves for past insults, real and imaginary. The remaining procession of men who wore the title of emperor in the West includes one, Majorian, who had the integrity, the ability, and the courage to have effected a reform of the Roman world but whose reforms were so unpopular that his achievements were forgotten. After a reign of five years, he was compelled to abdicate, and he died immediately afterwards. It is profitless to name the emperors who come between his reign and the abdication of the appropriately named Augustulus (little Augustus) in 476, which was the signal for the Roman senate to consent that the seat of "universal empire" should be transferred from Rome to Constantinople.

Within twenty years, nine emperors had been named, and all had failed to hold the ruins of the West. They were succeeded by the barbarian king Odoacer, who imposed a military pacification upon the exhausted kingdom of Italy between 476 and 490. It remained for Theodoric, king of the Ostrogoths, to restore a degree of prosperity to the Italian peninsula. The fate of the East was far different, and Gibbon reserves for his last three volumes the details of a thousand years of

Byzantine history. His last lament is for the decay of the Roman spirit, which was the "real" cause of Roman ruin. He looks back once again at the primitive purity of early republican days:

In the age of Roman virtue the provinces were subject to the arms, and the citizens to the laws, of the republic, till those laws were subverted by civil discord, and both the city and the provinces became the servile property of a tyrant. The forms of the constitution, which alleviated or disguised their abject slavery, were abolished by time and violence; the Italians alternately lamented the presence or absence of the sovereigns whom they detested or despised; and the succession of five centuries inflicted the various evils of military licence, capricious despotism, and elaborate oppression.

By contrast, the primitive virtues of the barbarians came to appear admirable.

At the end of the long account of Roman ruin, Gibbon artfully inserts a long, deliberately delayed chapter on the institution of the monastic life and the conversion of the barbarians to Christianity. The thirty-seventh chapter is the crown of the religious edifice which has been gradually built in the course of three volumes, as Gibbon related what he saw as "the progress, the persecutions, the establishment, the divisions, the final triumph, and the gradual corruption of Christianity." Moreover, the chapter shows some of the most important results of the success of Christianity which had been described in Chapter XXVIII, and it is a thematic as well as a structural counterpart to the earlier chapter. The first and shorter part of the chapter is expressive of Gibbon's entire contempt for the monastic ideal. By the monks, he says, every sensation that is offensive to man was thought acceptable to God; and he continually arraigns their asceticism as one of the most irrational forms of masochism. Their studies are said to darken, rather than to dispel the cloud of superstition; and the life of such a saint as Simeon Stylites, who lived on the top of a pillar in the Syrian desert for thirty years, excites only the contempt and pity of a philosopher like Gibbon. Such lives, he insists, serve no useful purpose.

The pride, wealth, and luxury found in some of the later monasteries are equally censured; and it is hard to refuse to one of the author's footnotes the smile which it was intended to provoke at the worldliness of the professedly religious: "I have somewhere heard or read the frank confession of a Benedictine abbot: 'my vow of poverty has given me an hundred thousand crowns a year; my vow of obedience has raised me to the rank of a sovereign prince.' I forget the consequences of his vow of chastity." The persecution of the orthodox or Nicene Catholics by the Arian Vandals does not give quite the same opportunities for irreverent comedy, nor does the conversion of the Goths.

In describing Ulphilas, the bishop and apostle of the Goths, Gibbon shows for his blameless life and indefatigable zeal something of that love and reverence which was accorded to him by his converts, who likewise admired him for practicing the truth and virtue which he had preached. The ground had been prepared for him, as for other missionaries, by the previous persuasions of the many Christians who had been taken prisoner by the barbarians and enslaved by them. Here Christianity is shown to have had useful effects, and it is therefore admired. There is no sneer in the sentences which describe the changes worked by the new religion in the conduct of the conquerors: "Christianity, which opened the gates of Heaven to the barbarians, introduced an important change in their moral and political condition. . . . In the most corrupt state of Christianity [they] might learn justice from the *law,* and mercy from the *gospel. . .*"; and there is no doubt that many of them did so; but the full flowering of Christian virtue was prevented by the horrid fact that Ulphilas was an Arian and a heretic and had induced most of the pagans to follow him in his religious beliefs.

It was in Africa that the most violent result of the consequent conflict between Arians and Catholics was to be seen. Genseric, king of the Vandals, was one of the least amenable of the barbarians; and he was a convert to Arianism. It is natural that he should have tolerated no difference of religious opinion from his own. Gibbon stigmatizes him and his successors as fanatics like the English Puritans of the Civil War and recounts with sorrow the savage persecution of the Catholic majority in Africa by the Arians under Genseric. But the Catholics were only too ready to retort in kind, and the two parties are held up to shame and obloquy; for, when the Catholic turn came to win royal proselytes and to claim the allegiance of the barbarians, they practiced similarly inhuman cruelties—physical and mental torture of their adversaries, deprivation of civil rights and of property, banishment and murder. With the success of the Catholic party, religious persecution declined; and only the Jews were left as prey for the spirit of persecution. Later periods found other doctrines to argue about and other reasons for the Catholics to persecute their Christian brethren. Gibbon promises here to relate in his Byzantine history the political influence of later religious disputes upon the decline of the Byzantine Empire. Meanwhile, we are to note the effects of the division of Europe into separate, barbarian kingdoms.

The thirty-eighth and last chapter of the third volume tells of the triumphs and conversion of Clovis, the establishment of the Franks as the ruling race in Gaul under this Merovingian dynasty, and the breakup of Gaul into small districts under the authority of those Frankish rulers who were strong enough to keep and extend a limited dominion. We learn also of the establishment of the institution of slavery and the nominal conversion of all the heathen to Catholic Christianity; but the savage passions of the Franks were literally ungovernable. Their strong sense of personal independence, based upon a consciousness of physical strength, "disdained the labour of government"; and they had no experience of the benefits of an elaborate and splendid civilization which might have persuaded them to establish a system of constitutional liberty. After the death of Clovis, his followers lapsed into anarchy; and Gibbon amuses himself by tracing from the Frankish spirit some of the characteristics of the modern French, of whom he writes: "It has been reserved for the same nation to expose, by their intemperate vices, the most odious abuse of freedom, and to supply its loss by the spirit of honour and humanity, which now alleviates and dignifies their obedience to an absolute sovereign." That the passage was published before the French Revolution only makes its singular penetration the more remarkable.

What the Franks neglected to do for themselves, the bishops of Spain were able to do for the Visigoths. Where the Franks yielded a captious and superstitious obedience to their clergy in religious matters, the Visigoths welcomed the peace, order, and stability which was introduced into the government of the whole state by the authority and example of their bishops. While Gibbon dislikes the style and detests the superstition of the Code of Laws established in Spain, he recognizes that it bears witness to a more civilized and enlightened state of society than that of the Franks. His account of the disorder of Britain is best passed over because he lacked, and he knew that he lacked, the materials to do justice to the task.

If we ask what lessons Gibbon intends his readers to learn from the first half of his work, the answer is given in a short conclusion to the third volume entitled "General Observations on the Fall of the Roman Empire in the West," which is an attempt to summarize the remarks upon the causes of the decline and fall which are scattered throughout the first three volumes. We may group the causes as follows: 1. The first cause was a loss of faith in republican virtue and honor, for which it is hard to find any anterior causes. The Romans seem simply to have lost faith in themselves and in their institutions. 2. Accompanying this loss, and perhaps as a result of it, a gradual change occurred from the more democratic forms of government under an elective senate and an executive chief magistrate to an ever more centralized government under the despotic control of a single emperor. 3. With the decline of independence went a refusal to give military service in person for the defense of the state; and the consequence was the rise of mercenary legions (who became a separate political power) and then of armies of barbarians paid in money or in booty, who quickly became aware of the weaknesses of the empire which they were supposed to be defending. 4. The immense size of the empire made it impossible to control or govern efficiently, and "the decline of Rome was the natural and inevitable effect of immoderate greatness." Many of the other evils stemmed from this fact: the attempt to govern effectively by dividing the empire led to an extension of what we would now regard as bureaucracy, to oppressive taxation, and to the extension of luxurious living by those who made the most of the uncertain present; and the establishment of despotism as an efficient way of controlling the new administration led to the abuse of power by the emperors and their servants. 5. The rise of Christianity encouraged the practice of the passive virtues and often led to an inactive and unproductive celibacy; it introduced new principles of dissension into the empire and increased civil strife (but it did mollify the ferocious temper of barbarian conquerors, and perhaps cushion the fall of the empire). 6. The Romans were unaware of the nature and extent of the barbarian movements outside the boundaries of the empire and did not therefore realize the extent of their danger, or prepare adequately to meet it.

Some of these causes have a decidedly modern ring to them—excessive centralization, an impersonal and irresponsible bureaucracy, and the concentration of power in the hands of a few people at the head of large organizations contributed to the downfall of the Empire. Modern man may choose, as he reads this *History*, to heed and act upon whichever of Gibbon's warnings he pleases; but he will have to be more successful than the emperors were.

VI   *The Holy City of Byzantium*

It was tempting, at this point, for Gibbon to take a holiday from the *History* and pretend that, with the fall of the imperial city which gave its name to the Empire, the history of Rome was really over. Gibbon did, in fact, take time to review his plan and materials afresh; for, if he had continued his work on the same scale as the first three volumes, he would have been obliged to write at least six volumes more—three for each of the two remaining periods into which he had at first divided the materials for his *History*; and the prospect was daunting, even to the industrious author, who gave the following reassurances: "The most patient reader, who computes that three ponderous volumes have been already employed on the events of four centuries, may perhaps be alarmed at the long prospect of nine hundred years. But it is not my intention to expatiate with the same minuteness on the whole series of the Byzantine history."

In 1782, when most of Gibbon's task was still before him, the highlights of Eastern history had seemed to be the reign of Justinian, the rise and conquests of the Mahometans, and those later conquests of the Crusaders and the Turks which are connected with the history of modern Europe. The period from the seventh to the eleventh century had not taken form in his mind; and, when he came to compose the last three volumes, it is plain that no such orderly progression, pattern, or series of contrasts had revealed itself to the historian as we have seen in the separate volumes of the first half of his work.

While there are suggestions in the grouping of the subjects of the fourth volume to indicate that Gibbon was still attempting to continue in the manner of the first three, when he comes to the last two volumes—the fifth and sixth—character, chapter, and theme are no longer amenable to a balanced, antithetical treatment. For the first time, the author is reduced to the expedient of dealing with each of the main assailants of the Eastern Empire in turn, according to a very elastic and approximate chronology. When, at the beginning of the fifth volume, he explains what he intends to do, he excuses himself by reference to "a tedious and uniform tale of weakness and misery . . . a dead uniformity of abject vices." With this view of the Byzantines, we cannot wonder at his seeking relief from their history in the livelier groups of Franks, of Arabs, of Bulgarians, Hungarians, and Russians who assail the Eastern Empire.

But the difficulty which he experienced with his unsympathetic and intractable materials rarely produces dullness in the narrative, and in some of his chapter arrangements he is able to follow a familiar and effective plan. The material is so arranged, for example, that the three chapters on the rise of Islam are succeeded by two chapters on the decline of the Eastern Empire and on the persecution of the Paulician heresy, which provide a spirited contrast. But the total impression of the last three volumes is weakened by the neglect of chronology, which makes it difficult to remember and to interrelate the incursions of the various troops of barbarians and Christians, for each chapter or group of chapters may cover a period of two to six hundred years. However, Gibbon never loses his grasp upon general ideas in the wealth of detail; and he relates the nations to one another, or anticipates future events, when to do so will illustrate a principle or maxim. The splendid peroration to the whole work provided by the last three chapters cannot conceal—though it certainly palliates—the comparative failure in these volumes of the power of architectural construction—of what Matthew Arnold called "architectonics." We may therefore be content with a description of the fourth volume as a whole and then of some of the more outstanding incidents and chapters from the last two volumes,—and, at the same time, be confident of doing no injustice to Gibbon's handling of the work as a whole.

Volume Four consists of nine chapters, XXXIX to XLVII; and it appears to open in the old manner with the brief antithetical paragraph: "After the fall of the Roman Empire in the West, an interval of fifty years, till the memorable reign of Justinian, is faintly marked by the obscure names and imperfect annals of Zeno, Anastasius, and Justin, who successively ascended the throne of Constantinople. During the same period, Italy revived and flourished under the government of a Gothic king who might have deserved a statue among the best and bravest of the ancient Romans."

The energetic and successful reign of this Christian and barbaric hero, Theodoric, is the main subject of Chapter XXXIX; and his virtues provide an admirable foil to the supposed weaknesses of the Eastern emperors whose reigns are so summarily dismissed. The historian's own humanity and civilization are reflected in his remarks that "The reputation of Theodoric may repose with more confidence on the visible peace and prosperity of a reign of thirty-three years, the unanimous esteem of his own times, and the memory of his wisdom and courage, his justice and humanity, which was deeply impressed on the minds of the Goths and Italians. ... The life of Theodoric represents the rare and meritorious example of a barbarian who sheathed his sword in the pride of victory and the vigour of his age." This open admiration is accompanied by an impartial appreciation of the hero's personal and political defects. In the first place, Theodoric is accused of a lack of vision, in that he adopted the system of government established by Constantine and his successors (and we know that Gibbon considered this expensive and decorative form of despotism to have been one of the main immediate causes of the downfall of the Empire); in the second instance, we are shown that he could be both jealous and cruel in persecuting for imagined offences those who, like Boethius, had served him long and faithfully.

One of the main distinguishing features of Theodoric's reign in Gibbon's eyes is undoubtedly the peaceful coexistence of an Arian king with an Athanasian people. Theodoric is represented as a statesman and a philosopher in his salutary indifference to religious superstitions; by contrast, the Catholics are accused of a scandalous venality in electing the Popes, and it is carefully insinuated that they were both cowardly and spiteful when we put together the facts that the Catholics "respected the armed heresy of the Goths" but persecuted the helpless, inoffensive Jews. Other touches of the old sprightliness are apparent in the remarks of the concluding paragraph upon the death of Theodoric, but there is a hint of the historian's dismay at the vast extent of the work yet before him; for, in one of the footnotes he confesses that he has "laboured" (this is his own significant word) to extract a rational narrative from the "dark, concise and various" hints obtained from four different historical sources. However, we continue to hear the unaffectedly rational Gibbon, the man of Good Sense, throughout the chapter, and most particularly in his warmly approving comments upon the philosophical conduct of Boethius in his varying fortunes.

By the laws of contrast at work in the previous volumes of the *History*, we might now expect a chapter on the weakness of an Eastern emperor, and it is indeed something of this kind that we are offered in Chapter XL. But the thirty-three years of Theodoric's reign in Italy do not provide the historian with such ample material as the thirty-eight-year reign of Justinian in the East, and four chapters are now given to the events of this period in Africa and Italy, as well as in the countries of the Danube and Persia. The effect of this fortieth chapter upon the reader is one of confusion. It describes the peaceful administration of Justinian in the East under seven heads; and the different sections are so amply, diffusely, and variously illustrated that it becomes quickly apparent how ill-founded were any expectations of a clear and deliberate contrast between Theodoric and Justinian in the manner of the first three volumes.

Three features of this chapter dispose us to feel that Gibbon has manipulated the facts into demonstrating his assertion that Constantinople adopted the follies, though not the virtues, of ancient Rome.

The first feature is his ample relation of the scandalous history of Empress Theodora: on the sole evidence of the *Secret History* of Procopius (whom Gibbon stigmatizes elsewhere as inconsistent and malign), he retails the infamous detail of her private life and its effect upon public affairs through her influence over the doting emperor. Modern authorities agree that the youth of Theodora was in general disreputable, without thinking it necessary to believe in the details; but Gibbon undoubtedly enjoys himself in using Theodora to discredit her husband. The second feature is his refusal to draw conclusions favorable to Justinian from the fact that he built elaborate frontier fortifications with which to protect from the barbarians an empire which was obviously populous, industrious in the arts of peace, and wealthy; for these precautions can have been neither so timid nor so fruitless as Gibbon implies. The third feature is the comparative tameness and inconclusiveness of a lengthy narrative for which the historian can find no splendid peroration. The chapter ends, fairly enough, by telling us that Justinian abolished the last trace of republican institutions, the consulship; and it ends accordingly with less of a bang than a whimper.

The forty-first chapter is the first of three in which the conquests and virtues of Belisarius, the greatest of Justinian's generals, are displayed; and it is the main chapter on this topic. His virtues as shown here would appear to make the light of the Eastern Empire shine, were it not that the weaknesses of the emperor are constantly intruded to dim its luster; even worse devices are employed to blacken the long tale of Belisarius's splendid victories over the Vandals in Africa and over the Goths in Italy, which seemed to have restored some of the power and the glory of the Roman Empire. In the previous chapter, the vices of Theodora were used to present the whole reign of Justinian in an unfavorable light; in this chapter, the dishonorable conduct of Antonina, the wife of Belisarius and the intimate friend of Theodora, is related to make the unconquerable patience and loyalty of Belisarius appear below or above that of a man. The conquest of Africa from the Vandals under Gelimer, the capture of Rome and its defense against the Goths, and the subjection of the whole Gothic kingdom of Italy are the triumphs of Belisarius which Gibbon admits; but he rewards them only by a coy, careful refusal actually to call Belisarius a cuckold, while amply demonstrating the fact that he is one. The last paragraphs of the chapter are hardly worthy of the historian, but the chapter as a whole has a sweep and command of materials—and of the reader's interest—which make it comparable with the best work of the earlier volumes.

In the two succeeding chapters Gibbon describes additional wars, conquests, and triumphs obtained by the generals of Justinian against the Persians and against revolt in Italy and Africa; but he insists that these (to use his own expressions) were the feeble and pernicious efforts of old age, which exhausted the remaining strength of the Empire and speeded its complete collapse. Certainly it is true that after the deaths of Belisarius and Justinian, Eastern attempts to reconquer and revitalize Rome were at an end; and, for our present purposes, we must overlook such interesting episodes as the military victories of the eunuch Narses in the renewed struggle with the Goths and the humane conduct of his adversary, the courteous and Christian Totila, in his wars against the Eastern generals.

The historical narrative is suspended during the whole of Chapter XLIV, which is a lengthy, erudite, and at the same time concise description of the development of the system of Roman Law up to the age of Justinian, one of the great reformers of the legal code. So accurate and ample is Gibbon's account that it was long used by lawyers as a standard text upon the subject. A chapter of such weight and authority would have formed a splendid center to a symmetrical arrangement of materials within this volume; but, as the volume now stands, the chapter only provides an ironic contrast with the breakup of the political system, which is described in the preceding and succeeding chapters. Of the three chapters which remain, two are devoted to the continuing ruin of the kingdom of Italy and to the attacks of the Persians upon the Eastern Empire; and the patience of the reader might well be exhausted by "the repetition of the same hostilities, undertaken without cause, prosecuted without glory, and terminated without effect" which, Gibbon says, would constitute the history of the Eastern wars. However, a variety of lesser heroes enliven these pages, from Tiberius II and the Lombard prince Autharis to Gregory the Great.

Some few remarks upon the effects of Christianity in the lives of the great hint at the subject of the last chapter of the volume. Of an emperor Gibbon writes: "During the last years of Justinian, his infirm mind was devoted to heavenly contemplation, and he neglected the business of the lower world"; of a cleric: "the pope asserted, most probably with truth, that a linen which had been sanctified in the neighbourhood of [St. Paul's] body, or the filings of his chain, which it was sometimes easy and sometimes impossible to obtain, possessed an equal degree of miraculous virtue." We may choose to remember the intent of such sentences as these when we discover that the forty-seventh chapter is a history of the various divisions which occurred within the Christian church between the years 400 and 1600 A.D. This chapter, whose placing was so much admired by Gibbon's best biographer, G. M. Young, is a fitting climax to the confusions of Byzantium, a fitting prelude to the confusions of the following volumes, and an interesting counterpart to the rise of Mahomet which is to be described in the fifty-first and fifty-second chapters. The excesses of the Christians prepare us for a friendly consideration of their enemies.

The forty-seventh chapter is a little less warm in its dislike of religious controversy than were previous chapters treating this subject. It outlines the theological history of the various beliefs concerning the doctrine of the Incarnation of Christ and concludes with a lengthy account of the progress of the Oriental sects which adopted and developed the different definitions of the faith, with the intention of demonstrating the important contribution of these dissensions to the downfall of the Eastern Empire. The controversies about the nature of the Incarnation are very carefully handled, but Gibbon makes no secret of his feeling that they are meaningless. His opinion of the five general councils of the church is adequately conveyed by his description of the first Council of Ephesus as "this episcopal tumult, which at the distance of thirteen centuries assumes the venerable aspect of the third œcumenical council."

He ridicules the faith of modern Christians in the decisions of such councils when, after recording an important decision of the Council of Chalcedon, he notes that their "infallible decree, after it had been ratified with deliberate votes and vehement acclamations, was overturned in the next session by the opposition of the legates and their Oriental friends." The only real success in defining doctrine is accorded to the Henoticon written by Emperor Zeno, and not to the work of any ecclesiastic; but Zeno's momentary victory is soon contrasted with the ridiculous partisanship of Justinian (according to Gibbon's metaphor, the first of the theological insects who "darted his sting and distilled his venom,") and all would-be definers of doctrine are made to seem equally ridiculous.

Indifference and contempt, rather than partisanship and mockery, are the historian's weapons in this chapter. Perhaps Gibbon's real difficulty is that he has neither sympathy nor understanding for controversies which appear to him meaningless except for their historical effects. Hostile to the Christians because their doctrines are rationally indefensible, he treats every evidence of humanity in their conduct with respect. In particular he admires Jesus of Nazareth because "He lived and died for the service of mankind." Socrates, he points out, had done the same; and both men deserve praise and respect for their practical humanity. But the mistakes of their followers are in danger of making their lives and examples meaningless, and those mistakes have continued into modern times. Gibbon speaks from the experience of a twice-converted man.

In the last chapter of Volume IV, the forty-eighth, Gibbon takes that final review of his remaining materials which we have already mentioned. The absence, loss, or imperfection of contemporary evidence about the period enables, and indeed almost obliges, him to compress within the pages of this chapter six hundred years of Byzantine history and the reigns of sixty emperors. The succession of pictures is as lively as it is bewildering, and it may perhaps justify the historian's solemn reflection that our immortal reason survives and disdains the crimes and follies of human ambition that has always been so eager, in a narrow span, to grasp at a precarious, short-lived enjoyment. A reader may well enjoy the rapid series of vignettes and the pithy comments upon them while he remains too bewildered to trace the connections between them.

There is a similar danger in reading the whole of the last two volumes: the portraits of the manners and conquests of particular nations are memorable, while the connection with the history of Byzantium which justifies their inclusion can only be remembered by the most careful reader. We may therefore consider only the outstanding episodes of Mahomet's rise to power as a fair sample of the writing which is clearly related to the religious theme of the whole *History.* Chapter XLIX, the first of Volume V, is devoted to the history and manners of the Franks, but Gibbon returns in Chapter L to this favorite theme: "While the state was exhausted by the Persian war, and the church was distracted by the Nestorian and Monophysite sects, Mahomet, with the sword in one hand and the Koran in the other, erected his throne on the ruins of Christianity and of Rome." But there were other reasons for the spread of the new faith; for Gibbon finds occasion to admire the good sense and unaffected humanity of the new leader and to approve the reasonableness of his creed.

Gibbon can hardly have confused the conduct of the Arab with that of an eighteenth-century gentleman, but he finds in the Mahometan creed an idea most congenial to nature and to reason: the unity of God. (We can see now why he had devoted so much careful attention to the

Christian quarrels over the nature of the Trinity—in order to be able to bring out their foolish fanaticism by the powerful contrast with the simple faith of the followers of Mahomet.) While Gibbon admires this part of the creed, he has the rational man's suspicion of its other essential tenet, which he regards as a pious fraud, or a manufacture of enthusiasm: "The faith which . . . he preached . . . is compounded of an eternal truth and a necessary fiction, THAT THERE IS ONLY ONE GOD, AND THAT MAHOMET IS THE APOSTLE OF GOD." But Gibbon is more charitable to the necessary fiction than we might have expected after his treatment of religions like the Christian and the Magian. He frequently praises the mixtures of reason and enthusiasm, of humanity and zeal, of rationality and revelation which he discovers in the conduct and the precepts of the new sectaries.

Nothing better explains the rationalism of Gibbon than the paragraph in which he accounts for the success of the prophet:

It is the duty of a man and a citizen to impart the doctrine of salvation, to rescue his country from the dominion of sin and error. The energy of a mind incessantly bent on the same object would convert a general obligation into a particular call; the suggestions of the understanding or the fancy would be felt as the inspirations of Heaven; the labour of thought would expire in rapture and vision; and the inward sensation, the invisible monitor, would be described with the form and attributes of an angel of God. From enthusiasm to imposture the step is perilous and slippery. . . .

The step is taken, probably by Mahomet, and certainly by his followers. Gibbon's distaste for their delusions is entertainingly shown in the cool impertinence of his comment upon one of the prophet's dreams: "Beyond the seventh heaven Mahomet alone was permitted to proceed; he passed the veil of unity, approached within two bowshots of the throne, and felt a cold that pierced him to the heart, when his shoulder was touched by the hand of God. After this familiar but important conversation, he again descended to Jerusalem. . . ." All sympathy for claims to supernatural knowledge must be dissolved in rational amusement. We may more seriously reflect that this method is the historian's favorite and most effective way of dealing with all pretensions to revelation: Hume would have smiled approvingly at so effective a use of irony for such a purpose.

There is no doubt in the historian's mind that the new religion was an improvement upon those which were at that time being preached and practiced in the Near East, and he accounts for the rapid spread of Mahometanism in the course of the Arab conquests by finding it purer than the system of Zoroaster, more liberal than the law of Moses, and less inconsistent with reason than "the creed of mystery and superstition which, in the seventh century, disgraced the simplicity of the Gospel."

In the three chapters upon the Arab expansion which follows the spread of Mahometanism, Gibbon sustains and excites the reader's attention and interest by his accounts of Arab customs, by the vivid descriptions of their conquests, and by his demonstration of their active virtues. When he returns, briefly, to Byzantium in the fifty-third chapter, he dwells upon the decay of taste and genius, the want of national emulation, and the imperfections of the Greeks. This chapter is balanced and complemented by the next, which describes the supine superstition of the Greek church and the spread of the Paulician heresy, from which Gibbon traces with approval the roots of a more modern, more reasonable Protestantism. Liberty of conscience, the practice of religious toleration, and the liberalization of the laws are the gradual gains of many centuries of human progress and experience. But the fifth volume is almost entirely concerned with the successes of the Mahometans; and it ends, suitably enough, with the conquest of Jerusalem by the Turks.

With his next great subject, the Crusades, Gibbon has no sympathy: to describe them is only, for him, to trace the dismal effects of fanaticism; and his description of them suffers from his feeling that each crusade is only a repetition of the same causes and effects, though the individual episodes which he selects are exciting and some of the digressions are curiously informative. We would not be without his accounts of Saladin and Richard I, and we may share his absorption in the pedigree of the Courtenays. But the main interest of the Crusades must be that they produce a Christian sack of Constantinople in 1204, and show us the irony of the partially civilized barbarians pillaging New Rome. He hurries us on, however, as he feels he must, through the last days of the Eastern Empire and the pressures of the latest bands of barbarians, the Moguls and the Tartars, to the last religious quarrels between East and West, and to the long-awaited cataclysm, the final capture of Constantinople by the Turks, under Mahomet II.

The three final chapters of the whole work form a decorative ending by returning us to the history of the first Rome in the Middle Ages and by showing how the Popes obtained their secular and religious dominion. A final attack upon the vices of ecclesiastical government as exemplified in the Popes closes the penultimate chapter and leaves the seventy-first and final chapter to pronounce a temperate elegy over the ruins of ancient Rome as they appeared in the fifteenth century at the date of the fall of Constantinople.

The foregoing survey of the subject matter and construction of the *Decline and Fall* may help to show that its sheer mass has a carefully delineated outline and a proportion between its various parts which are not dictated by historical considerations alone. The splendid and entertaining unity of the work is maintained above all by its elevated and rational tone, by the confidence with which it appeals constantly to the judgment of the humane sentiments of the educated man. Even where the modern reader may not be in sympathy with particular interpretations of historical fact, or less sure than the eighteenth century that rationality is the sole test of truth, he responds to Gibbon's humanity, shares his amusement at the follies of mankind, is informed by his careful marshaling of fact, and respects the consistency of his judgments. The historian's detachment and the arrangement of his matter show that he views history as a kind of philosophical teaching by example.

CHAPTER 3

The Humane Philosopher

I *Conversation and Common Sense*

AN understanding of Gibbon and a liking for his work is best obtained by reading the *Autobiography*. Any biographer of Gibbon must draw heavily on this work in order to give a true picture of the man, and reference to the notes shows how much the preceding sketch of his life is dependent upon Gibbon's own account. The other main source of our knowledge comes from the letters which he wrote to his friends and relations. The letters are usually unstudied and comparatively informal in manner when he is asking for information or discussing his money affairs; but they, like his published works, slip naturally into a more polished, mannered, and dignified style when he indulges himself in abstractions and in philosophical meditations. Both these sources give a picture of the man which is reflected in the underlying assumptions of the *History*.

The *Autobiography* as we know it was compiled, after the historian's death, by his friend Lord Sheffield by a conflation of the five separate versions of *Memoirs* which he had found among Gibbon's papers. The assembling of these into a fluent narration was a work of art and a labor of love, and the resulting volume shows us the man whom his contemporaries knew so well, with an imposing company manner (which had become so natural to him that he could not leave it off) and a decent respect for the susceptibilities of others which modified the ironic vein of which he was master. A pleasant little story has been handed down to us by George Colman of an occasion in his youth when the great Dr. Johnson had been rather brusque with him in company: "Mauled as I had been by Johnson, Gibbon poured balm upon my bruises, by condescending, once or twice, in the course of the evening, to talk with me; the great historian was light and playful, suiting his manner to the capacity of the boy; but it was done *more suâ*, still his mannerism prevailed; still he tapped his snuff-box; still he smurked, and smiled, and rounded his periods with the same air of good-breeding, as if he were conversing with men."[1]

The secret of Gibbon's success as a writer was that he cultivated the art of conversation until it was no longer artifice but second nature for him to present thoughts so well digested and observations so well phrased that he wrote as he spoke and spoke as he wrote with the engaging politeness, the authoritative elegance, and the memorable antithetical weightiness of an affable archangel. His enemies may have felt that he could make balance sheets sound like Homer—and Homer sound like balance sheets—or as one contemporary put it ". . . we are too often reminded of that great man Mr. Prig, the auctioneer, whose manner was so inimitably fine, that he had as much to say upon a ribbon as upon a Raphael";[2] but they were complaining of the habits of thought which made the splendid and complicated unity of the *History* possible.

Gibbon was perfectly well aware of his own mannerisms. In the *Autobiography* he tells us that, before he wrote, he would arrange a whole paragraph in his mind to hear what it sounded like and then he would think it over and polish it before committing it to paper (185). Maria Holroyd, who wrote so disrespectfully of the oracular pronouncements of the "King" of Lausanne (see p. 42 above), thoroughly enjoyed his conversational style, which she recognized in the parts of the Memoirs which were read aloud by Lord Sheffield to his family while he was preparing the *Autobiography* for print; and she felt a severe pang at the thought that she would never again hear his amusing, instructive conversation.[3] For the formality of his language was no mere mannerism: it was a means of conveying thought and feeling with precision and control.

Many later critics have thought that Gibbon showed a deficiency of human feeling in his description of the way in which he fell in love, but this is, in fact, a remarkable demonstration of his delicacy of touch. This well-known passage (part of which is quoted on p. 14 above) is an excellent introduction to the style of the man and of the age. We should recall that it was written some thirty years or more after the events which it describes; that the author was remembering the most poignant experience of his youth; and that he could expect mature readers to appreciate and judge his youthful self from his own standpoint of late middle age. Given this information, the sentiments could hardly have been expressed with greater nicety:

I hesitate, from the apprehension of ridicule, when I approach the delicate subject of my early love. By this word I do not mean the polite attention, the gallantry without hope or design, which has originated in the spirit of French chivalry, and is interwoven with the texture of French manners. I understand by this passion the union of desire, friendship, and tenderness, which is inflamed by a single female, which prefers her to the rest of her sex, and which seeks her possession as the supreme or the sole happiness of our being. I need not blush at recollecting the object of my choice; and though my love was disappointed of success, I am rather proud that I was once capable of feeling such a pure and exalted sentiment (82).

The paragraph shows that Gibbon was still self-conscious, still sensitive, still tender about the experience. His reflections upon the passion of love are just: he does not ignore physical desire, but he sees it in the perspective of polite custom and of the civilizing emotions, friendship and tenderness. He was capable of "the gross appetite of love" only when it was elevated into what he termed sentimental passion and what we may call delicate feeling.[4]

The transformation of the historian into the human being is no less convincing because the language is elevated. The experience of having loved and lost was an enrichment of his life: such is the implication of his language and cadence. At the age of fifty, he is too self-controlled to indulge romantic passion by a romantic extravagance of language, but in his very negatives—"disappointed of success"—there is an autumnal wistfulness which is equally appealing. As we observed earlier, the conclusion of his idyll when he met his father was not so abrupt as the language of the *Autobiography* suggests and the fatal words, "I sighed as a lover: I obeyed as a son," attempt to disarm criticism of the young man's conduct by admitting it. Gibbon is letting us know that he too could see the ludicrous (but still to him painful) gap between aspiration and achievement, between romantic passion and common sense.

The *Autobiography* is full of common sense so uncommonly well expressed that it qualifies, by Pope's definition, as wit. A capacity for fine distinctions, an ability to display striking resemblances, a niceness in handling the language, and a perception of the incongruous help to explain the close association between the words "wit" and "humor" in more modern usage. If there is not, as a recent critic has suggested, a laugh in every line,[5] there is certainly a smile on every page. Sometimes his wit is sardonic, occasionally sarcastic and even quietly cynical, betraying the author's confidence in the superiority of his own rationality: more often it is excited by a just observation of human nature, a humane regard for his fellows, a benevolent concern for the general welfare, or a reasoned and reluctant acceptance of the vagaries of human folly. Always the language is decorous, but often, lurking behind the decorum, is an unpleasant reality: when the contrast between expression and fact is most marked, Gibbon's irony or innuendo asserts most effectively the standards of eighteenth-century civilization.

His vision of academics, steeped in port and prejudice among the "monks" of Oxford, is comic because it implies the contrast between the virtues which ought to have been possessed by a band of celibate scholars and the slothful neglect of their duties in favor of the mildly discreditable vices of body and intellect which they practiced. This particular phrase gains a great deal of its force from the total picture of Oxford which Gibbon delineates with all the incisiveness of a Hogarth. His strictures upon the "sallies of religious phrenzy" which he finds in the respectable works of William Law are convincing mainly because his own language is consistently moderate in tone. The description of his own father as a man who "had always preferred the highest and the lowest company, for which he was equally qualified" has that sting in its tail which compels recognition of an unpleasant truth having ill consequences for the son, without involving the latter in any lengthy condemnation of the father whom he had respected and loved. The statement that the pleasures of a "town life are within the reach of every man who is regardless of his health, his money and his company" contains his judgment upon the civilized life which he finds so comfortable and so pleasing. This use of the implications and connotations of words and phrases for the setting of standards of taste and judgment is Gibbon's universal practice; and the full impact of the manner is only to be appreciated through the cumulative effect of such phrases within the whole work.

The quotations in the previous paragraph may persuade the reader to share or to repudiate the pleasures of rational superiority, but they give only half the picture of their author. Formality of language does not conceal the warmth of Gibbon's attachments to his family and friends, and in particular to his father, his aunt, his stepmother, Deyverdun, and Holroyd. He calls his attachment to his stepmother a "warm and solid" one, which indeed it was; and he comes very near to using the language of enthusiasm when he speaks of his enduring friendship with Deyverdun. During the summer months which they spent together at Buriton, they enjoyed free conversation "on every topic that could interest the heart or understanding, [which] would have reconciled me to a desert or a prison" (*Autobiography*, 161–62).

Gibbon's reasoned approval of moderation is well shown in his praise of Swiss society where "the decent freedom of both sexes is equally remote from the extremes of simplicity and refinement" and "the invisible line between liberty and licentiousness was never transgressed by a gesture, a word, or a look" (*Autobiography*, 133). Gibbon does not write in this way simply from a love of antithesis: he feels the solid advantages of distinguishing between extremes and of picking with care that middle path which is suited to particular circumstances.

It is now pertinent to examine the ways in which Gibbon embodies the standards of rational moderation in the *Decline and Fall*. If, in the words of his third chapter, history is "little more than the register of the crimes, follies and misfortunes of mankind," what good reason can there be for recording them? The historian's own short answer to the question is given in Chapter XVI: history "undertakes to record the transactions of the past for the benefit of future ages." Gibbon would never have agreed with the old paradox that history teaches us that history teaches us nothing, for it is everywhere evident in the *Decline and Fall* that the barbarity of the past should make us admire the civilization of the eighteenth-century present. In passage after passage of the *History* we are invited to enjoy the ironic, the well-nigh comic, contrast between the refined language which Gibbon uses and the brute facts which it conveys. When, for example, the Goths have besieged and captured Trebizond, pillaged it, and massacred the inhabitants, we are told that they were "satisfied with the success of their first naval expedition [and] returned in triumph to their new establishments in the kingdom of Bosphorus." The two words "satisfied" and "establishments," with their polite connotations of gentility and the well-ordered and wealthy eighteenth-century household, contrast oddly—as they are meant to do—with the fury of the barbarians and with the primitive life of a tented encampment. From such descriptions we derive the amusement and instruction which Gibbon believes to be the products of a good history.

The reading of history is one of the resources of the leisured gentleman, and Gibbon intends it to contribute to the civilizing process in his own century. As he reminds us in the fifteenth chapter, "The acquisition of knowledge, the exercise of our reason or fancy and the cheerful flow of unguarded conversation may employ the leisure of a liberal mind"—and the historian's own liberality is shown in a large variety of ways. The first of these is his careful historical method. When, for example, he has to choose between differing authorities in order to write about an incident in the life of Theodosius, he decides that the truth may be found in a just medium between two extreme and contradictory assertions. A similar practical and pragmatic fairness in the use of his sources is a principle with him, and the rational processes by which he assesses the reliability of historical testimony demonstrate a constant philosophical liberality of mind. He felt the support of a common sense which was based upon the common consent of the cultivated part of mankind, of men who thought and felt like himself.

To use the adjective "philosophical" of Gibbon or of the *History* is not to imply that he was an academic philosopher. The one contemporary British philosopher whom he mentions with approval is, not unnaturally, Hume, whose rationality offers him the support of several footnote references when superstition is to be denounced or enthusiasm ridiculed. It is to Hume, therefore, that we shall go in order to understand the basis of some of the historian's attitudes. Gibbon makes a distinction between the object of real philosophy, which is to him "the knowledge that is suited to our situation and powers, the whole compass of moral, natural and mathematical science," and the objects of metaphysical speculation, which he considered to be the figment of a fevered brain and a waste of the reasonable man's time. To him, philosophy most often means either natural and experimental philosophy (what we call "natural science"), or simply the powers of reasoning and rationalization, in so far as they produce serenity of outlook and equability of temper. Natural philosophy he approves of heartily, for it is the application of common sense to the observation of natural phenomena and the systematization of such observations in order to give us the benefits of applied science. In this respect, Gibbon is a distant but faithful disciple of such experimental philosophers as Bishop Sprat and other early members of the Royal Society.

It is the cultivated common sense of a gentleman which obliges Gibbon to write with dry indignation of the way in which the superstition of the monks gradually extinguished the hostile light of philosophy and science. He perpetually contrasts the prejudices and partiality of fanaticism with the observations of common sense and reason. What he considers the liberal motives of reason and humanity produce the toleration of his *History*. One vice only is to him inexcusable—the refusal to be liberally minded, the vice of fanaticism itself—for even common sense may be powerless against the enthusiast. As he remarks in the chapter which records the division of the Empire, "Philosophy alone can boast (and perhaps it is no more than the boast of philosophy) that her gentle hand is able to eradicate from the human mind the latent and deadly principle of fanaticism." He sees that pagans and Christians alike have violated the natural obligations of humanity and justice under the excuses of policy or religion, but how far public safety or any other consideration may operate to dissolve these obligations is a doctrine of which he himself desires to remain ignorant.

Gibbon's humanitarian sentiments have a truly philosophic nobility; but he, like most of us, is irritated by what he cannot understand, and attempts therefore to explain it away. When we come to his views of other people's religion, we find them largely negative. In the fifteenth chapter he observes that in his own day "a latent and involuntary scepticism adheres to the most pious dispositions [whose] admission of supernatural truths is much less an active consent than a cold and passive acquiescence." Here we have the Gibbon of the *Autobiography*, who acquiesced with implicit belief in the tenets and mysteries which are adopted by the general consent of Catholics and Protestants. Religious creeds are unimportant so long as they result in conduct which is useful, generous, and humane. But he demonstrates again and again to his own satisfaction how dangerous are the religious metaphysics which so soon degenerate into superstition, and he constantly opposes the evidences of common sense and natural science to the testimonies of miracle and revelation.

His central assumption in metaphysical matters is implicit in this sentence from the fifteenth chapter: "every friend to revelation is persuaded of the reality, and every reasonable man is convinced of the cessation, of miraculous powers." This opposition of the enthusiast (for that, surely, is what we are to understand by the expression "friend to revelation") to the reasonable man is the mainstay of his attack upon religion. It is the contradiction of common sense which he resents so hotly, and his own experience of religious controversy explains this reaction. As a result of his explorations into the arguments for and against the doctrines of the Roman church, which were pursued with conscientious devotion over several of his most ardent youthful years, he had come to the conclusion that good works are more important than faith.

Consequently, the useful virtues of a practical Christianity receive everywhere the tribute of praise in the *Decline and Fall*. Like the prudent magistrate of Constantine's day, any eighteenth-century rationalist might "observe with pleasure the progress of a religion which diffused among the people a pure, benevolent and universal system of ethics, adapted to every duty and every condition of life, recommended as the will and reason of the Deity, and enforced by the sanction of eternal rewards and punishments." Gibbon feels that the will of the Deity whom he can recognize is remarkably like the reason of the ordinary well-educated man. He is, therefore, particularly averse to anything which might be termed miraculous; and, when he comes to religious history, he is confident that "the frequent repetition of miracles serves to provoke where it does not subdue the reason of mankind."

By experience, reading, observation, and upbringing, Gibbon had become the sort of philosopher who would examine with calm suspicion "the dreams and omens, the miracles and prodigies" of both secular and religious history; and, like such a philospher, he did undoubtedly conclude that the appearance of miracles (which he was occasionally disposed to concede) was necessarily the result of deliberate fraud, of unconscious self-deception, or of pious literary manufacture. "Every event, or appearance, or accident," he remarks, "which *seems to deviate from the ordinary course of nature* [my italics] has been rashly ascribed to the immediate action of the Deity." The *History* is amply sprinkled with remarks, innuendos, and inferences which support this rational view of miracles. As far as Gibbon is concerned, there are two possible explanations of events which seem to deviate from the ordinary course of nature: either they did not happen (though we have been deceived into believing that they did, by enthusiasm or by the errors of the senses); or else they did happen, but upon more careful examination will be found not to contradict natural law.

When he is confronted with the evidences for the miraculous vision of Constantine, he properly considers the reliability of the historical testimony — the relevant pages are dotted with his footnotes — and then concludes that "the protestant and philosophic readers of the present age will incline to believe that . . . Constantine attested a wilful falsehood by a solemn and deliberate perjury." But his contempt for superstition is not confined to Christianity; his sneer at "a seasonable vision (for such are the manufacture of every religion)" is directed at the followers of Mahomet. In regard to miracles and visions, the *History* has the merit of complete consistency. All phenomena which eighteenth-century science cannot account for are rejected with philosophical impartiality: the miracles of the saints, the Zoroastrians, the Mahometans, or Attila are made to appear equally ridiculous.

What Gibbon never does face is the possibility that the laws of nature may be other than his kind of common sense assumes them to be. It is, however, open to us to observe that what appears extraordinary to one age may be unremarkable to another; that the concept of the natural varies with time, custom, and experience; and that scientific law is itself in a state of constant modification as new facts are discovered and as reinterpretations of fact are made. It is more open to us than it was to him to be "superstitious" and to allow for the existence of what we cannot perfectly comprehend in our picture of the universe and of the nature of man. However, Gibbon could not and would not admit the possibility of a reality in which the miracle was not an infraction of natural law, but a demonstration of an underlying order different in kind and quality from that which he could understand.

The invariability of human nature and of natural law is as truly a philosophic principle with Gibbon as it is with Hume, and the *History* reminds us frequently that men are expected to think and behave similarly in all ages. Gibbon approved heartily of Hume's description of the nature of personal merit, which he thought to consist entirely in the possession of qualities "useful or agreeable to the person himself or to others."[6] Hume disapproves of what he considers the monkish virtues of celibacy, fasting, penance, mortification, self-denial, humility, and solitude because they "serve to no manner of purpose" — they do not enable a man to get on in the world or make him more valuable to his fellows. Indeed, such so-called virtues seem to Hume to be vices; and he feels sure that no saint (Hume calls such a man a gloomy harebrained enthusiast) would ever be admitted into intimacy and society "except by those who are as delirious and dismal as himself." The social virtues, on the other hand, have a natural grace and amiability. Preconceptions such as these account for Gibbon's jeers at "the painful celibacy of ecclesiastics" and at monastic virtue which "is painful to the individual and useless to mankind." His accounts in Chapter XXXVIII of the lives of the early monks are entertaining and scornful, intended to excite only the reader's contempt and pity. Yet it is really the extravagances of some believers and not the entire body of religious thought which he despises.

Religion has, in fact, an honored place in the *History* and in

Gibbon's private philosophy. In describing the system erected by the Emperor Julian (who had been brought up on freedom, liberality, and paganism), Gibbon remarks that his "theological system appears to have contained the sublime and important principles of natural religion." When we ask what is the "natural religion" which the historian appears to endorse, there is no immediate answer. His clearest declaration of faith consists of the sentence, "The God of nature has written his existence on all his works, and his law in the heart of man." The meaning of this declaration is in part elucidated by his remarks upon the rational enthusiasm of Mahomet, who adored "an infinite and eternal being, without form or place, without issue or similitude, present to our most secret thoughts, existing by the necessity of his own nature, and deriving from himself all moral and intellectual perfection."

Such a God was too abstract to commend himself to the historian's imagination, however; and his rational admiration (not his adoration) is reserved for the God whom he calls the Great Artificer of the universe. This admiration[7] is to be noted in such asides as his comment upon the magnificence of the church of Santa Sophia: "how dull is the artifice, how insignificant is the labour, if it be compared with the formation of the vilest insect that crawls upon the surface of the temple." Natural religion, then, would seem to consist in the admiration of natural phenomena which man cannot reproduce or imitate, and in the acceptance of a universe governed by the laws of natural science. With this concept goes the implication that phenomena as yet unexplained are explicable in such terms. Admiration of the useful and the beautiful in man and in nature then becomes a religious activity.

There is a frequent insistence upon the benevolence and reliability of nature and natural phenomena which helps Gibbon to view man in perspective; and his remarks upon comets and earthquakes are illuminating in this connection. The highly decorated sentence upon the seventh recorded appearance of the comet Electra in the year 1680 demonstrates the reaction of an enlightened age to such phenomena: "The philosophy of Bayle dispelled a prejudice which Milton's muse had so recently adorned, that the comet 'from its horrid hair shakes pestilence and war.' Its road in the heavens was observed with exquisite skill by Flamsteed and Cassini: and the mathematical science of Bernouilli, Newton and Halley investigated the laws of its revolutions." Gibbon foresees with pleasure that the astronomers' calculation of a reappearance of this comet in the year 2355 may be "verified by the astronomers of some future capital in the Siberian or American wilderness."

Even when he is describing the most destructive earthquakes, he can contrast the comparatively benevolent impartiality of nature with the self-interested passion and violence of man: "The historian may content himself with an observation, which seems to be justified by experience, that man had more to fear from the passions of his fellow creatures than from the convulsions of the elements." The pessimism of such a comment is amply supported by the events of the *History*, and there can be no doubt that many of his subjects give him reason for it; but he knows that he has as much to hope as to fear from the complicated web of human thoughts, motives, and feelings.

II   *Politics and Progress*

This balance of hope and fear in his own mind is particularly nice when he is thinking about the various ways in which men have been governed. In frequent comments and asides he reveals his feelings about the forms of government which are best adapted to the fulfillment of human needs—and here he parts company with the great mouthpiece of his century, Alexander Pope. The sentiments of the couplet "For forms of government let fools contest / Whate'er is best administered is best" might tempt, but they would never convince, Gibbon; for he was willing to trust to the workings of reason, in the minds of those men who can feel its influence, to produce the most practicable form of government. In general, he distrusted democracy, admired oligarchy, and felt that a limited constitutional monarchy like that of eighteenth-century Britain offered man the greatest chance of earthly happiness: democratic government only works when small numbers of well-informed people are involved in the choice of the principles upon which their rulers or governors shall act.

The outstanding example in the *Decline and Fall* of such successful self-government is a small episode in the total *History*—the retreat of the Ten Thousand Greek soldiers who had been left to their fate in Asia Minor after the death of Cyrus in the middle of a military expedition. The contrast between the eternal weakness of despotism and the strength of democracy in this particular case shows why Gibbon could admire these Greeks and yet distrust egalitarianism: "Instead of tamely resigning themselves to the secret deliberations and private views of a single person, the united councils of the Greeks were inspired by the generous enthusiasm of a popular assembly, where the mind of each citizen is filled with the love of glory, the pride of freedom and the contempt of death." This is not always, or often, Gibbon's opinion of the effectiveness of popular assemblies; but the Ten Thousand were helped by the comparative smallness of their numbers and driven by the immediacy of their danger to the effective practice of the democratic virtues. Because the Greeks knew themselves accurately and recognized their real superiority in arms and discipline, "they disdained to yield, they refused to capitulate [and] every obstacle was surmounted by their patience, courage and military skill."

Such examples of successful democracy are rare, and Gibbon stigmatizes as a specious and popular maxim (he uses both adjectives with a very exact sense of their meaning) the belief that every citizen has an equal right to enact the laws which he is bound to obey. Like the prudent usurper Augustus, Gibbon is convinced of the mischief of popular assemblies and of the futility of expecting good government or useful laws to emerge from the popular vote. In such circumstances he has every reason to fear the dominion of "the wild democracy of the passions" and to oppose it to "the perfect aristocracy of reason and virtue." For even an absolute monarch like Augustus can bring happiness to his people if his conduct is rational. It is very easy to see why Gibbon should feel this so strongly when we read about the way in which the legions came to "elect" a long series of bad and ineffective emperors by disorderly acclamation. Popular democracy of this kind is no better than mob rule, and it is only productive of worse disorder for, as Gibbon says, "under a democratical government the citizens exercise the power of sovereignty; and these powers will be first abused, and afterwards lost, if they are committed to an unwieldy multitude." To such disorder even despotism is preferable, but Gibbon has his own third alternative which, as one might expect, is a happy medium between the two extremes.

In his comments in the third chapter upon the reign of Augustus, the reader can see this practical compromise most clearly. He writes of a martial nobility and stubborn commons—an oligarchy which will fight for its property and form itself into elective assemblies, and which will thereby persuade a monarch to maintain representative government. Augustus is his topic, but modern constitutional monarchy is his theme. Had he not been able, in his own Continental travels, to contrast the rigid etiquette and repressive government of the courts of Naples and Sardinia with the rational freedom which could be enjoyed by an English gentleman at home? And was not this freedom far more glorious than the splendid despotism of ancient Rome? His practical illustrations of the advantages of constitutional monarchy convince him of the superiority and rightness of things as they are in Great Britain under the Hanoverians.

No one can see better than he that the principle of a hereditary monarchy may easily be held up to republican ridicule—but he can also see that the institution works. He therefore expects that our more serious thoughts "will respect a useful prejudice that establishes a rule of succession, independent of the passions of mankind"; and, in view of what he can show us in the tumultuary elections of ancient history, he expects also that we "shall cheerfully acquiesce in any expedient which deprives the multitude of the dangerous, and indeed of the ideal, power of giving themselves a master." As a result both of historical and of personal experience, Gibbon concludes that a hereditary monarchy is the most useful and least dangerous method of succession and form of government: "The superior prerogative of birth, when it has obtained the sanction of time and popular opinion, is the plainest and least invidious of all distinctions among mankind."

In other words, Gibbon believed that, although popularly elected assemblies are incapable of choosing suitable rulers, the assembly itself provides those checks and balances upon the arbitrary will of a hereditary monarch which make monarchy tolerable and effective as a form of government. He sums up his own satisfaction with modern constitutional monarchy in the concluding observations to the first half of his *History* as follows: "The abuses of tyranny are restrained by the mutual influence of fear and shame; republics have acquired order and stability; monarchies have imbibed the principles of freedom, or, at least, of moderation; and some sense of honour and justice is introduced into the most defective constitutions by the general manners of the times."

The enunciation of common-sense principles which provide an acceptable political middle way is, of course, a generalization from eighteenth-century European practice (and, in particular, from English practice) which, when applied to the history of ancient Rome, conveniently highlights the inadequacies of republican and of imperial rule. The dangers of despotism are illustrated in the histories of the other great peoples in whom Gibbon is interested. It is of the decay of the power and empire of the Caliphs that he remarks, "So uniform are the mischiefs of a military despotism, that I seem to repeat the story of the Praetorians of Rome." The Roman system of government is only freely admired when, as under Nerva, Trajan, Hadrian, and the Antonines, it approximates most closely to the pattern of English constitutional government; in fact, these reigns seem to Gibbon to have been the only period of ancient history during which the happiness of a great people was the sole object of government. A lurking suspicion may nevertheless remain in the reader's mind that Gibbon has a warm admiration for the successful despot.

It was not only in the organization of government that the eighteenth century was superior to the ancient past. At the end of his celebrated peroration to the third volume of the *Decline and Fall*, Gibbon declares what is implicit in the tone of the whole work—namely, his faith in the possibility, even the necessity, of continuous progress; his conviction that "every age of the world has increased, and still increases the real wealth, the happiness, the knowledge, and perhaps the virtue of the human race." Evidences of his belief in the superiority of the moderns in the useful arts, manners, letters, painting, war, commerce, and conduct are scattered throughout the *History*. He ranks Isaac Newton with Homer and Cicero; thinks the paintings of Raphael and the sculpture of Alessandro Algardi equal to the works of their great Classical predecessors; exalts the researches of Archbishop Usher above the "rubbish" of the Dark Ages; distinguishes the native graces of La Fontaine (and the concise elegance of his Classical model, Phaedrus) from the incredible and clumsily narrated fables of India; admires the superiority of Classical to Oriental literature; ascribes almost equal merit to the rational philosophies of Voltaire and of Hume in contradistinction to the superstition of religious writers of the past; and compliments George III on his interest in the arts and sciences which led him to found the Royal Academy and to patronize Captain Cook's bloodless and blameless voyages of discovery. All these comparisons seem to Gibbon to provide evidences of modern man's superiority to the civilizations which have preceded his own; and those earlier civilizations in their turn were evidences of man's slow ascent from savagery and barbarism to that refinement and politeness which give meaning to modern life.

In his guise of philosopher Gibbon considers the whole of Western Europe as one great republic, all of whose inhabitants have attained a similar level of politeness and cultivation and enjoy a similar state of happiness. The laws, arts, and manners of the individual nations may be distinguishable from one another; but there is a generally high standard of civilization which enables him to compare the state of modern Europe very favorably with the happiest periods of ancient history. He feels that Germany, in particular, shows a marked and splendid development from a wilderness of forest and marshland into a country of walled towns and flourishing industry; even Russia appears to him a powerful and civilized Empire; and pre-Revolutionary France commands the highest admiration. To the essential practical bases of a flourishing agriculture, ingenious and useful manufactures, and a prosperous commerce, modern France, he thinks, adds the graces which may be found in the most elegant capital city of the world. In the last sentence of Chapter XIX Gibbon asks himself what the Emperor Julian would think of Paris if he were to revisit it now, and he concludes in a triumphant triplet of praise that "he might converse with men of science and genius, capable of understanding and of instructing a disciple of the Greeks; he might excuse the lively and graceful follies of a nation whose martial spirit has never been enervated by the indulgence of luxury; and he must applaud the perfection of that inestimable art which softens and refines and embellishes the intercourse of social life." Gibbon must surely have savored the ironical flavor which the Revolution was later to give to his praises.

The French may be the masters of the finest arts of civilized life—and among these the art of conversation may be chief—but amongst all the nations of Europe similar civilized advantages are shared as the result of an age-long process which started when men first learned to use and control fire and first learned to develop the mechanical skills which followed from the invention of the wheel. Gibbon knows that the fine arts cannot flourish without the useful arts, and he always attaches the first importance to these foundations of peace and prosperity. He is as delighted as Addison was before him to praise the civilizing force of trade; to rejoice that extensive commerce demonstrates the interdependence of the nations of the world; and to await with complacent satisfaction what he regards as the eventual and inevitable consequence of commerce—the dissemination of Western culture throughout the savage parts of the globe.

He notes with pleasure that man's more barbarous habits and instincts have been softened and civilized by the refinement of modern manners. Even war, that perpetual violation of humanity and justice, has now some contingent advantages since advances in the science of waging war may lead to a proportionable improvement in the arts of peace. Mathematics, chemistry, mechanics, and architecture have all been applied to the service of war and all have received some advantages through this service. However, when remarking on the rapid spread of the knowledge of the uses of gunpowder, he comments soberly: "If we contrast the rapid progress of this mischievous discovery with the slow and laborious advances of reason, science and the arts of peace, a philosopher according to his temper, will laugh or weep at the folly of mankind."

On the other hand, he believes that the fear of war has contributed to the preservation of personal valor and national courage; and, most important of all, he notes that in his own day wars are no longer fought all over the homelands of the combatants. Indeed, he finds a cause for self-congratulation in the fact that military operations "are conducted on a distant frontier by an order of men who devote their lives to the study and practice of the military art: the rest of the country and the community enjoys in the midst of war the tranquillity of peace, and is only made sensible of the change by the aggravation or increase of the public taxes." A twentieth-century man may well wonder at this confidence and may contrast Gibbon's easy years in the militia and his careful skirting of the borders of enemy France with his own liability for military service in a foreign theater or the all-embracing destructiveness of global conflict.

Well may Gibbon feel that he is better off as an eighteenth-century gentleman than he would have been as a Roman emperor or an Ottoman caliph. In a delightful footnote to Chapter LII, he declares that his own hours of enjoyment have far exceeded those of the great Caliph Abdalrahman (who said that he could only count fourteen happy days in his fifty-year reign), and he expects that his own happiness will be long continued. There was good reason to acknowledge in the *Autobiography* that he had drawn a high prize in the lottery of life in having been born in a free and enlightened country of an honorable and wealthy family. But this happy lot was not the lot of all, nor did he expect it to be; we may note this important limitation upon his praise of his own times, that the enjoyment of the greatest prosperity is limited to a small élite.

CHAPTER 4

The Image of His Mind

I *A Judicial Manner*

IT was once said by a reader of Gibbon's *Autobiography* that the author did not know the difference between himself and the Roman Empire. Gibbon himself thought that a writer's style should be "the image of his mind." As we have seen in previous chapters, Gibbon's style does embody what may best be called his philosophy of life, and it was this philosophy which was the real object of the attacks made upon his style after his death. Men of the late eighteenth century were, like Lord Chief Justice Mansfield, prepared to call his style "abominable", and a nineteenth-century admirer called his sentences majestic and monotonous. Our own reading may reverse such adverse verdicts. Gibbon's style is formal, but it conveys with accuracy and precision the refinements of an educated sensibility and the deliberative judgments of a rational mind.

We have seen how the actual form of the *History*, the arrangement of chapters and volumes, results from and embodies the historian's evaluation of his materials; and we must now ask how the smaller elements are organized and constructed to contribute to the total impression. In doing so, we are accepting the account of his method of composition set down in the *Autobiography*: "It has always been my practice to cast a long paragraph in a single mould, to try it by my ear, to deposit it in my memory, but to suspend the action of the pen till I had given the last polish to my work." We can hardly doubt that each paragraph was conceived as a part of the whole chapter or that each sentence was intended to work with its fellows in qualifying and building up the particular and general effects of the narration. If Gibbon did do exactly what he says he did, and the *History* gives us every reason to believe him, he possessed a remarkable memory as well for the cadences as for the matter of his work. What we must now try to do is to see him working downwards, not only (to use G. M. Young's perceptive expression) from the theme to the chapter and from the chapter to the paragraph, but also from the paragraph to the sentence, and from the sentence right down to the single epithet.

The commonest form of ordering in the *History* is that weighing of opposing or complementary ideas which is embodied in antithesis. This conveys a Gibbonian habit of thought which is no mere stylistic device but a method of judgment. The flexibility of use and variety of meaning which he can convey by means of antithesis are best illustrated by quotation. In its simplest form an antithesis may run: "The grateful legions served the emperor while living, and revenged him when dead." This statement impresses by the apparent completeness of idea, pithiness of expression, and finality of manner. In a more refined form it may read, "To resist was fatal and it was impossible to fly." Here the touch of epigram is reinforced by the chiasmus or grammatical inversion of the statement. Or the sense may be reinforced by the repetition of a key word in the comparison: "It has been observed, with ingenuity, and not without truth, that the *command* of iron soon gives a nation the *command* of gold [my italics] ." The curtness of statement is removed by the qualification of the first verb.

The lengthening out of the antithesis has happy effects which may be heard in the reading of the following sentence, where the natural speech stresses are marked in order to show how the rhythmical repetition decorates the contrast: "Their progress was checked by the want of arms and discipline and their fury was diverted by the intestine division of ancient Germany." Gibbon's prime concern here is so to order the information as to make it melodious, memorable, and palatable. Sometimes he achieves a perfect rhythmical equivalence which comes near to verse. The final terms of a sentence about the barbarism of Sarmatian manners condemn them for using poisoned weapons, and the condemnation is emphasized by the regularity of the rhythm:

> since a people impressed with a sense of humanity
> would have abhorred so cruel a practice,
> and a nation skilled in the arts of war
> would have disdained so impotent a resource.

The parallel is exact, and it intensifies our abhorrence of crude and savage cunning.

An even more precise formal perfection is attained in the unkind judgment upon the life of Constantine:

> As he gradually advánced in the knówledge of trúth
> he propórtionably declíned in the práctice of vírtue.

Here the rhythmical parallel serves to paint an ironic contrast, and we find Addisonian elegance allied to Baconian conciseness to produce the distinctive philosophical weight of the later eighteenth century. If we compare this sentence with a rather longer one, we shall find that the heightening of interest by rhythmical means can have a more sophisticated effect:

> The usual numbers of consuls, praetors and tribunes
> were /annually invˈested with
>   their respéctive énsigns of óffice
> and contínued to dischárge some
>   of their léast impórtant fúnctions.

The rhythmical equivalence of the last two clauses of this sentence extends to the unstressed as well as to the stressed syllables, and it reveals its insidious point only in the last words, whose significance is momentarily disguised by the falling cadence and the regular rhythm. The powerlessness of the consuls is the subject of the sentence, but it is disguised by the measured magnificence of the rhythm. Could sound be a better echo of sense?

Time and again the putting together of a pair, or of several pairs, of ideas has the effect of pointing a moral as well as of adorning the tale. Gibbon's rational scorn for the tumultuary "elections" of emperors by the soldiers is frequently conveyed by a succession of critical antitheses:

> On the fírst néws of the émperor's déath
> the troóps expréssed some suspícion and reséntment,
> till the óne was remóved and the óther assuáged
> by a donative of twenty pieces of gold to each soldier.
> They then ratified the election and acknowledged the merit
> of their new sovereign.

A large part of the effect of this passage lies in the rhythm of the four separate sections of the first sentence. The reader's suspicions are lulled by the repetition of four stresses in each of the first three sections—the third providing the most perfect pattern—until, quite suddenly and unexpectedly, the true facts of the situation and the real motives of the soldiers are revealed in the totally different and quite matter-of-fact rhythm of the fourth and final section. The succeeding sentence, with its different rhythmic balance, then carries the full force of innuendo: a whole battery of weaknesses is held up for tacit condemnation—greed, suspicion, resentment, susceptibility to crowd emotion and narrow self-interest—without Gibbon's needing to make a single comment; the reader is intended to be amused and edified by this exposure of the moral weaknesses of the troops. The passage is, in fact, a piece of effective satire upon vice and folly.

Gibbon ventures upon satire in all its degrees within the *History*, and antithesis is one of his favorite methods of conveying all shades of reprobation, from insinuation and innuendo to sarcasm and invective. When he remarks that "The protéction of the Rhaétian fr/ontier, and the persec/ution of the C/atholic church, det/ained C/onstantine in I/taly," he is not only balancing good conduct against evil, but he is also suggesting that the persecution of the Catholics was some sort of protection for the Empire. Half the fun of the sentence lies again in the contrast between the rhythmical and syntactical equivalence of its first two clauses and the shift of stress in the third. Later, he links together in the mind of the young Julian "The names of Christ and Constantius, the ideas of slavery and religion," in order to imply a real connection between the founder of the Christian religion and the crafty emperor, between Christianity and slavery, and between religion and Constantius. Gibbon deliberately mixes conventional ideas about Christianity for the purpose of making the reader question them.

But the Gibbonian antithesis is not always used with ulterior motives. It should be viewed rather as a way of marshaling the materials, of communicating information clearly and concisely, and of involving the reader with subtlety and precision in the patterns of historical fact which make the judgments of the *History* seem inevitable. It is part of the process of "exact identification of causal, temporal and other relations by means of grammatical form" which Yvor Winters admires in Hume's history.[1] When we turn from the sentence to the paragraph, we can see that Gibbon's frequent use of antithesis is no mere stylistic trick and that its use has not become so habitual as to deaden our responses. His summary of Roman policy towards the Germans illustrates this ordinary manner well. It is here arranged on the page in rhythmical units, to underline the artifice of the writing:

> They deemed it a much safer expedient
> to divide // than to combat the barbarians,
> from whose defeat they could derive
> neither honour // nor advantage.
> The money and negotiations of Rome
> insinuated themselves into the heart of Germany,
> and every art of seduction was used with dignity
> to conciliate those nations
> whom their proximity to the Rhine // or Danube
> might render the most useful friends //
> as well as the most troublesome enemies.
> Chiefs of renown and power //
> were flattered by the most trifling presents,
> which they received either as marks of distinction //
> or as the instruments of luxury. . . .
> Every quarrel among the Germans //
> was fomented by the intrigues of Rome,
> and every plan of union and public good //
> was defeated by the stronger bias of private jealousy and interest.

Abstracted from the paragraph, the pairs of opposing terms are plain enough: divide and combat; honour and advantage; money and negotiations; useful friends and troublesome enemies; union and public good versus private jealousy and interest. There is little to surprise and much to reflect upon in them as the repeated antitheses emphasize the divisive influence of Rome. The weight of the syntax and the accumulation of clauses, as well as the meaning of the words, show the Romans at their least attractive. The neglect of rhythmical equivalence—even where it could have been achieved but is not—("every plán of únion and públic goód" could have been balanced by "strónger bías of jéalousy and prívate ínterest") emphasizes the discords which the Romans work to achieve. This care for his speech tunes and rhythms brings the art of Gibbon's prose close to the art of eighteenth-century verse.

Before we embark upon a study of the Gibbonian triplet, it is useful, for the sake of comparison, to cite an example of the plainer, more natural-seeming manner which does not embody a constant series of antitheses for dignity or decoration. The paragraph in which Decius revives the office of censor shows a style of great flexibility, considerable speed, and complete lack of irony:

At the same time when Decius was struggling with the violence of the tempest, his mind, calm and deliberate amidst the tumult of war, investigated the more general causes that, since the age of the Antonines, had so impetuously urged the decline of the Roman greatness. He soon discovered that it was impossible to replace that greatness on a permanent basis, without restoring public virtue, ancient principles and manners, and the oppressed majesty of the laws. To execute this noble but arduous design, he first resolved to revive the obsolete office of censor; an office which, as long as it had subsisted in its pristine integrity, had so much contributed to the perpetuity of the state, till it was usurped and gradually neglected by the Caesars. Conscious that the favour of the sovereign may confer power, but that the esteem of the people can alone bestow authority, he submitted the choice of the censor to the unbiassed voice of the senate. By their unanimous vote, or rather acclamations, Valerian, who was afterwards an emperor, and who then served with distinction in the army of Decius, was declared the most worthy of that exalted honour.

What is noticeable about such passages is the high degree of abstraction in the language: a modern reader almost requires that the author shall tell him in the second sentence how public virtue was shown in an earlier period; what principles and customs had been lost; which majestic laws were now being infringed or forgotten. A sufficient reply to such questions has, in fact, been given many times over in the incidents of the *History* already recounted; and Gibbon is more conscious than we are of the usefulness and the necessity of generalizations and of the wealth of meaning and concrete experience which may be subsumed beneath abstractions. If his earlier rhythmical effects put the perceptive reader in mind of Pope's poetry, the use made of generalization (but not the manner) may remind him of Johnson's.

In the second sentence of the paragraph just quoted, Gibbon uses a tripartite construction; and the triplet is a basic element of his style. In its simplest form, it echoes Caesar: "they met, they saw, they encountered," or "They saw, they envied, they tasted the fertility of Crete"; and it can be even more dramatic and succinct: "Rufinus fell, groaned and expired." It can give an air of satisfying completeness to a statement: the manners of the Goths were "polished by time, education, and the influence of Christianity"; and it can convey a devastating distaste and an important moral judgment in one word: "those haughty troops . . . were distinguished by their gold collars, liberal pay, and *licentious* privileges" (my italics.) A more developed example of this device is contained in this brief description of the royal welcome for a hero: "Mascezel was received at the court of Milan with loud applause, affected gratitude and secret jealousy." In such a sentence, the sudden torque from praise to envy, which hinges on the tension of the second term "affected gratitude," has all the effect of savage satire.

Sometimes a progression of three nouns or verbs speeds or dramatizes the incidents of the narrative: Honorius is rescued from a besieged city by "the fame, the approach, and at length the presence" of Stilicho, whose reputation and generalship are conveyed by the rapidity of this progress and by the evident effect of his name upon the enemy. There is more obvious artifice in the claim that the mischievous Andronicus had "a heart to resolve, a head to contrive, and a hand to execute." Alliteration is not a device very frequently used in the *History*, and here it is only a handmaid to the verbs which give the sense of the whole man (all of a piece in *h*eart, *h*ead and *h*and) energetically engaged in his own amusement and aggrandizement. We move nearer to the full Gibbonian music and period where the triplet of verbs is extended and qualified in passages of narrative: "Antony, an illiterate youth of the lower parts of Thebais, distributed his patrimony, deserted his family and native home, and executed his monastic penance with original and intrepid fanaticism." In such a sentence the lengthening rhythms of successive clauses give an air of inevitability to the progress of the statement, and the coupling of two approving adjectives with "fanaticism" underlines the surprise which even the historian feels at the unexpected combination of qualities in the hero.

Particularly in the paragraphs of summation, sentences tend to be organized in groups of three coordinate clauses; and, in the following examples, taken from the conclusion of the thirty-sixth chapter, describing the miserable state of Italy under Odoacer, we find an increasing grammatical elaboration in each successive clause which helps to pile on the agony:

> In the division and the decline of the empire, the tributary
> harvests of Egypt and Africa were withdrawn;
> the numbers of the inhabitants continually diminished with
> the means of subsistence;
> and the country was exhausted by the irretrievable losses
> of war, famine and pestilence.

A consistently more elaborate sentence from the same paragraph runs:

> The plebeians of Rome, who were fed by the hand of their
> master, perished or disappeared as soon as his liberality
> was suppressed;
> the decline of the arts reduced the industrious mechanic
> to idleness and want;
> and the senators, who might support with patience the
> ruin of their country, bewailed their private loss of
> wealth and luxury.

The variation of mood between the clauses is as remarkable as the grandeur of their effect. Should we pity the plebeians for the loss of their livelihood or scorn them for their parasitic dependence? We simply note, as a matter of information, the plight of the industrious mechanic; but we must censure the short-sighted self-pity of the senators; and we feel that the satirical bite of the last clause is conveyed by the sharp antithesis of sentence structure and of idea.

For grander or calmer effects, the tripartite sentence may be stretched out even farther without losing any of its clarity or sacrificing truth to elegance. The conduct of the philosopher Libanius at the court of Julian is an excellent case in point:

> Instead of pressing, with the foremost of the crowd,
> into the palace of Constantinople,
> Libanius calmly expected his arrival at Antioch,
> withdrew from court on the first symptoms of coldness and indifference,
> required a formal invitation for each visit,
> and taught his sovereign an important lesson,
> that he might command the obedience of a subject, //
> but that he must deserve the attachment of a friend.

Again the last of the coordinate main clauses (this time four in number) concludes with an antithesis; but this time it is calmly presented and meticulously balanced, a reasonable reflection without innuendo or underhand motive. In a succeeding sentence, a similar structure is preserved in a reversed and modified form; it starts with a compressed and critical antithesis and concludes with two quartets, one of nouns and the other of verbs, in order to contain the full pith of the historian's praise and meaning:

> Julian might disdain the acclamations of a venal court
> who adored the imperial purple;
> but he was deeply flattered by the praise, the admonition,
> the freedom, and the envy of an independent philosopher,
> who refused his favours, loved his person, celebrated
> his fame, and protected his memory.

Any Gibbon lover will enjoy his own investigations into the almost unlimited variations upon the basic patterns of the author's sentences; and there is no doubt that, even when the famous style was no longer popular, its qualities were admired and utilized by writers of the next century. The power of organization which is shown in the elegant but lengthy triplet; the impressive certainty of the resounding phrase; the appearance of objectivity in the antithesis—all these are devices which continued to appeal to, and to be used by, historian, novelist, and politician in the succeeding age.

When we read the rhetorical climax in Disraeli's *Sybil*, "Two nations; between whom there is no intercourse and no sympathy; who are as ignorant of each other's habits, thoughts and feelings, as if they were dwellers in different zones, or inhabitants of different planets; who are formed by a different breeding, are fed by a different food, are ordered by different manners, and are not governed by the same laws" we may perhaps recall the less florid, less fervid, and better ordered model for Disraeli's cadences which Gibbon provides in his own description of the monks in Palestine: "The philosophic eye of Pliny had surveyed with astonishment a solitary people, who dwelt among the palm trees near the Dead Sea; who subsisted without money; who were propagated without women; and who derived from the disgust and repentance of mankind a perpetual supply of voluntary associates."

Gibbon also shows an enthusiasm for some of his minor heroes which would not have disgraced Thomas Babington Macaulay. The splendid *Times* obituary style of the description of Manuel is one of the best examples. The simplified historical parallels, the mythological analogy, and the excitement of the rapid narration look forward to the later period:

Educated in the silk and purple of the East, Manuel possessed the iron temper of a soldier, which cannot easily be paralleled, except in the lives of Richard the First of England, and of Charles the Twelfth of

Sweden. Such was his strength and exercise in arms that Raymond, surnamed the Hercules of Antioch, was incapable of wielding the lance and buckler of the Greek emperor. In a famous tournament he entered the lists on a fiery courser, and overturned in his first career two of the stoutest of the Italian knights. The first in the charge, the last in the retreat, his friends and enemies alike trembled, the former for *his* safety, the latter for their own.

This passage has all the simplified rhetoric of Macaulay's Third Chapter on the courtly captains, or of Motley's panegyric upon William of Orange. Gibbon's splendid, simplified black-and-white morality some-times sounds more like a nineteenth-century novelist than like the voice of eighteenth-century reason.

It is, nevertheless, reason which is the main force behind Gibbon's use of literary devices. The ambition to judge justly and humanely is conveyed in the irony and the antitheses of his style, and Gibbon steps aside many times in the *History* to remind us that even historical truth may lie exactly in the middle of two extremes. What he remarks about Julian is repeated with variations about many of the major and minor characters of the *History*: "We enjoy the singular advantage of comparing the pictures which have been delineated by his fondest admirers and his implacable enemies." But it would be mistaken to imagine that for Gibbon truth always lies in the just mean between two extremes, or that impartiality involves impassiveness. In many of the passages so far cited, the author's own emotional attitudes may be distinguished by the discerning reader; and we may profitably remem-ber his description of the emperor Honorius as a man who was without passions and *consequently* without talents.

II   *The Prose and the Passion*

What evidence of Gibbon's own passions is there in the *History* to confirm our impressions of his talents? And if we can detect passion, of what kind is it? If we except traces of what Richard Porson described as a "rage for indecency" (he has perhaps the history of Theodora particularly in mind), Gibbon's emotions are all on the side of humanity, moderation, and reasonable conduct. But in the occasional footnote we may detect a note of personal animus or of praise. "In his way Voltaire was a bigot, an intolerant bigot," declares one note; in another, Johnson is castigated for a mistaken opinion. Such signs of a petty passion are rare, even in the footnotes; in fact, some of his happiest comic and satirical sallies are to be found there. He enjoys italicizing the anomaly when, in recounting the massacre of seventy-one thousand intended brides, "John Trithemius presumes to mention the *children* of these British virgins," and he delights in telling us that "in the hands of a popular preacher an earthquake is an engine of admirable effect."

His emotional bias is most apparent in his asides upon superstition, which are almost invariably the most amusing; and two of these must do duty for many. He notes the story of a Catholic martyr who had carried his severed head in his hands for a considerable way and recalls that, of a similar tale, Madame du Deffand had observed "La distance n'y fait rien; il n'y a que le premier pas qui coûte." (The distance is unimportant; it's only the first step which matters.) Equally bland, and perhaps equally insouciant is his footnote upon earthquakes and inundations: "Epidaurus must have been overwhelmed, had not the prudent citizens placed St. Hilarion, an Egyptian monk, on the beach. He made the sign of the cross; the mountain-wave stopped, bowed and returned." These trivia are amusing, but it is fairer to him to remember that the notes bear constant witness to the meticulous care of his scholarship; he tries to account for the smallest factual detail, which is woven with careful elegance into the intricate web of his style.

As we have seen, the style is capable of the most graceful and purposeful modulations; and it may now be helpful to indicate the way in which Gibbon modulates in tone from innuendo and ordinary irony right up to the cold fury of sarcasm and invective. At the level of aspersion and innuendo, it would be easy to collect from almost any chapter of the *History* an anthology of entertaining examples, and many of the instances of stylistic devices cited above would qualify for inclusion. In the course of a few quotations it will become apparent how often the innuendo is directed at ordinary human follies and vices, and in particular at those of the great. The accumulating weight of the following sentence shows Gibbon using his sentence structure to underline the implied criticism of his victims' ridiculous complacency: "As soon as the consuls had discharged these customary duties, they were at liberty to retire into the shade of private life, and to enjoy during the remainder of the year the undisturbed contemplation of their own greatness." Here several aspersions are piled upon one another in Gibbon's happiest manner, but he can make just as telling an effect with the use of one word which promotes immediate reflection, as when he tells us that by the victorious Scanderbeg "the Ottoman garrisons were *indulged* in the choice of martyrdom or baptism" (my italics). The statement works, of course, to make us question not only the humanity of the indulgent victor but also the customs of religion. Perhaps here we are already over the narrow line which distinguished innuendo from irony proper.

Very often a single word in a sentence conveys the oblique hint of something amiss. During the last years of Justinian, we are told, "his infirm mind was devoted to heavenly contemplation." It is, of course, the collocation of the two adjectives which suggests to us that only the feebleminded are concerned with spiritual realities and that religion is a form of insanity. Either adjective, without the presence of the other, would have been harmless. Often, one adjective is enough. When Lucillian is massacred at Rheims "in an accidental mutiny of the Batavian cohorts," it is the very casual nature of the tragedy which is laconically and almost comically underlined by the adjective.

One of the words which Gibbon most often uses to convey an aspersion is the harmless adjective "seasonable." In his hands it repeatedly becomes the agent of insidious suggestion, as he points out "the merits of a seasonable conversion," the political uses of a "seasonable earthquake," the program of conquest supported by a "seasonable revelation," and the "seasonable aid" of visions and miracles in confirming the authenticity and powers of the most suspicious relics. No longer does the word mean simply "at the proper time"; it has taken entirely its secondary and dangerous significance of "opportune," with all the modern connotations of opportunism and of chicanery. A study of the *History* will show other similarly dangerous adjectives, amongst which "supine," "disappointed," and "specious" are some of the most active.

Supine is always a danger signal: a fit of "supine indifference" or security inevitably presages the sack of a city or the downfall of a people, and it almost always conveys a hint of comedy. Barbarians are guilty of a "supine indolence," and the defenders of Trebizond lose their city to the Goths in a fit of "supine negligence." But what, we may ask, had laid such different peoples flat on their backs—for this is what supine means? Certainly, at Trebizond, the numerous garrison were "dissolved in riot and luxury." The single word "dissolved" gives away the unpleasant fact which is concealed in the language of decorum; obviously, the garrison was dead drunk. Under such circumstances, it is no wonder that they "disdained to guard their impregnable fortifications." Our amusement at this statement is not only that of the philosophical onlooker upon human follies but also that of the literary stylist who can appreciate the fine irony of the verb "disdained" as applied to troops in this condition. It is such innuendoes as these that Boswell must have had in mind when he suggested that Gibbon "should have warned us of our danger, before we entered his garden of flowery eloquence, by advertising, 'Spring-guns and man-traps set here.' "[2]

Oblique hints, allusive remarks, and amusing aspersions make up the Gibbonian tale of suggestion and innuendo, thereby maintaining an atmosphere in which the reader must be ready to seize upon the slightest appearance of ambiguity as evidence of the author's attitudes and feelings. A word is enough to illuminate the tale of fact with a racy spark of opinion, and we do not need to share all the opinions in order to be able to enjoy Gibbon's expression of them. The sheer artistry of the method is a delight in itself. If we sometimes see irony where the author intended none, expectation is the best guide to a full understanding of the meaning of the *History*.

The ironies are not, of course, purely verbal. Gibbon's comment upon the personal quarrel between Boniface and Aëtius shows him, as he so often is, aware of the irony of Fate: "The republic was deprived by their mutual discord of the service of her two most illustrious champions." The sentence is a comment upon the folly of the republic and upon the folly of human passions which work blindly to produce results the opposite of those which might have been expected. This sort of irony is most frequent when religious matters are concerned. We find that the first Christian missionaries in Spain appealed to the evidence of reason and claimed the benefit of toleration: "But no sooner had they established their spiritual dominion than they exhorted the Christian kings to extirpate, without mercy, the remains of Roman or barbaric superstition." The simple putting together of the two facts is enough to expose the inhumanity of the missionaries; and Gibbon anticipates, with calm confidence, our assent to his implied comdemnation. The contradictions inherent in human character are the constant objects of Gibbon's comment, implicit and explicit; and a fair summing up of the chief reasons for his ironic treatment of so much passion is provided|in his comment upon the character of Motassem after the siege of Armorium: "To a point of honour Motassem had sacrificed a flourishing city, two hundred thousand lives, and the property of millions. The same caliph descended from his horse, and dirtied his robe, to relieve the distress of a decrepit old man, who, with his laden ass had fallen into a ditch. On which of these actions did he reflect with the most pleasure when he was summoned by the angel of death?"

What, we may ask with Falstaff, is the value of such honor? And how true is it that mankind is deceived by mere names? One of the chief purposes of Gibbon's irony is the promotion of such philosophical reflection. Such irony has a moral intention and effect.

The clearest irony of statement is often seen in the comments upon the behavior of his actors. When the Moguls conquer the cities of Asia, Gibbon describes in some detail the inhumanities which were their ordinary practice, and he concludes, "Such was the behaviour of the Moguls when they were not conscious of any extraordinary rigour." He relies upon our humanity, upon our very different point of view, to pass a judgment where he only states a horrifying truth.

Very occasionally vice and folly move Gibbon to open sarcasm or to the self-betraying emotions of invective, as when he comments that ecclesiastical writers are "apt to despise the profane virtues of sincerity and moderation," or when he stigmatizes the pulpit as "that safe and sacred organ of sedition." But the emotion is rarely sustained for as much as a sentence at a time, and it is frequently attributable as much to the historian's sources as to any animus of his own. Rarest of all in Gibbon is the open sneer. Occasionally an unlovely smirk contorts the face of the historian's muse, as when he reckons among the immediate followers of Arius "two bishops of Egypt, seven presbyters, twelve deacons, and (what may appear almost incredible) seven hundred virgins," or remarks in a footnote, "it can scarcely be supposed that the assembly of the bishops of Egypt would solemnly attest a *public* falsehood." It was Archdeacon William Paley who lamented the impossibility of refuting a sneer, and such examples explain why a reading of Gibbon should have prompted this reflection.

Gibbon's use of the English language has survived two hundred years of changing speech remarkably well, but the connoisseur will notice with pleasure some minor peculiarities of word usage which he shares with his century. "Prevent" is normally used in the sense of going before or anticipating or making unnecessary: "The fortunate soil assisted, and even prevented, the hand of cultivation . . ."; "the senate wisely prevented the clamours of the people, by the institution of a regular pay for the soldiers . . ."; "the prefect obeyed and even prevented the cruel mandates of the tyrant." Other interesting oddities are indicated by the words italicized in the following sentences quoted at random from the *History*: "*conciliating* [reconciling] the qualities of a soldier with those of a philosopher . . . the birth of Mahomet has *illustrated* [made illustrious] the province of Hejaz . . .

the defects of evidence were diligently *supplied* [compensated for] by the use of torture .... the baths were open for the *indiscriminate* [undiscriminating] service of the senators and the people .... Mr. Hume betrays some secret disposition to *extenuate* [make thinner] the populousness of ancient times .... he *insensibly* [without anyone noticing] discovered his new opinions." Such exact use of words in senses derived from their Classical origin imparts an occasional quaintness of flavor and a most pleasing reminder that we are in the eighteenth century.

A less noticeable feature of the style of the *History* is the use of metaphor. One of his least characteristic sentences is the explanation of his refusal to delineate in detail the eighteen varieties of Arian creed because "It is amusing enough to delineate the form, and to trace the vegetation, of a singular plant; but the tedious detail of leaves without flowers and of branches without fruit, would soon exhaust the patience and disappoint the curiosity of the laborious student." The familiar antithetical forms of this sentence do not entirely conceal the unfamiliar extension of a simple metaphor, and it is amusing to find Gibbon judging the growth of Arian sects by the standards of a living organism. As usual, the comparison is insidious; for the "singular plant" is metaphorically shown to be neither useful nor beautiful. In other contexts he insinuates the unnaturalness of Christianity with variations upon the same metaphor. In Persia, for example, "Christianity had struck a deep root, and the nations of the East reposed under its salutary shade." Of the decay of the Oriental members of Nestorian Catholicism, he writes, "These remote branches are long since withered; and the old patriarchal trunk is now divided." It is certainly significant that the memorable metaphors and similes refer so frequently to religious history.

The range of metaphorical reference is limited. One of the favorite implied comparisons is the pejorative reference to the swarming of flies or of locusts: "Under the warm influence of a feeble reign they [the official spies] multiplied to the incredible number of ten thousand ... the swarms of monks who arose from the Nile, overspread and darkened the face of the Christian world ... the number of eunuchs could be compared only with the insects of a summer's day." But Gibbon never descends to vulgar abuse, and he is happier with the implied metaphor than with the comparison fully explored. When he tells us that the mind of Athanasius was "tainted by the contagion of fanaticism," the insidious associations of corruption and disease attach themselves almost imperceptibly to our estimate of the abilities and mental capacities of the great prelate.

Often Gibbon amuses himself and instructs his readers by embodying his own feelings in the metaphors which he has found in his original sources. During the joint reigns of Maximian and Diocletian, we are told, the latter "enjoyed the comparison of a golden and an iron age, which was universally applied to their opposite maxims of government." The metaphor is then improved, from the same sources, into a mythological comparison which extends the ideas of the original metaphor and gives Gibbon the opportunity for an aside of rational skepticism: "From a motive either of pride or superstition, the two emperors assumed the titles, the one of Jovius, the other of Heraclius. Whilst the motion of the world (such was the language of their venal orators) was maintained by the all seeing wisdom of Jupiter, the invincible arm of Hercules purged the earth from monsters and tyrants." Such a passage gives us a clue to the reasons for Gibbon's distrust of metaphor: it is most often the language of flattery, of self-delusion, and of enthusiasm. With one important exception, he uses metaphor most confidently when he uses it least literally.

The exception is provided by what is, perhaps, his most frequently employed group of metaphors, the group concerned with armies and with battle. Undoubtedly such imagery was forcible to Gibbon because his military service and his reading in contemporary authors kept the physical reality of eighteenth-century methods of warfare present in his mind. When he wrote in the *Autobiography* of his ecclesiastical adversaries, and when he wrote in the *History* of the church as an army and of ecclesiastics as military officers, these metaphors were intended to represent his sense of moral conflict. But in Gibbon the conflict is often ironically viewed, and the battle metaphors are not so much heroic as mock-heroic.

In writing of the effect of the fifteenth and sixteenth chapters upon the English public, he declares "the shaft was shot, the alarm was sounded"; and he says that he was attacked by clerical critics, a victory over whom would be humiliating. Continuing the metaphor, he claims that "every polemic, of either University, discharged his sermon or pamphlet against the impenetrable silence of the Roman historian." Nevertheless, Dr. Priestley "threw down his two gauntlets . . . and continued to fire away his double battery." Gibbon was startled "by the first discharge of ecclesiastical ordnance" but found that it was an empty noise. The metaphorical arms, alarms, arrows, and cannon are meant to cast ridicule upon the militant clergy. The metaphors are all the more effective because they are the stock eighteenth-century language for dramatizing the moral struggle within the self. Gibbon awards himself a moral victory in awarding himself a military one.

In the *History*, the military analogies are often very subtly handled. Gibbon often insinuates that worldly ambition, and not a proper sense of vocation, animated many of the Christians who chose ordination. In the following sentences, he achieves this result by reminding us constantly of the military organization while writing about the ecclesiastical (the italics are mine):

The *office* of priests, like that of *soldiers* or magistrates, was *strenuously exercised* by those men whose temper and abilities had prompted them to embrace the ecclesiastical *profession* . . . . The whole body of the catholic clergy, *more numerous, perhaps, than the legions*, was exempted by the emperors from all service, private or public . . . which pressed on their fellow citizens with intolerable weight; and the *duties* of their holy *profession* were accepted as a full *discharge* of their *obligations* to the public.

Throughout the long paragraph of which this quotation is a part, the church is inferentially shown for what in Gibbon's mind it is: an armed band within the state, one of more effective power, influence, and internal discipline than the legions themselves. The dangers which Gibbon foresees in these swarms of ecclesiastics prevent the tone of this procession of metaphor from being merely mocking; it is designed to awaken the reader to an awareness of the increasing influence of the church upon the fate of the old Empire.

In such a chapter as the forty-seventh, military metaphors have a curious ambiguity of function. Some sentences are only metaphorical: the author declines in one of his footnotes to "enrich" his ignorance with the "spoils" of his learned predecessors. The opening paragraph, however, foreshadows a religious war of two hundred and fifty years which will abound in "clamorous or sanguinary contests"; and it is with something of a shock that we realize that Gibbon is writing the literal truth: the sectaries who are anxious to guard, and jealous to defend, particular doctrines will defend them not only through the ordinary medium of debate and argument but also with violence and bloodshed. The transformation from metaphorical description of arguments to factual description of real battles has the effect of making us share the historian's unfavorable view of Christian controversies. When Cyril of

Alexandria urges his flock to attack the unarmed and unprepared Jews, the Christians level the synagogues to the ground; and "the episcopal warrior, after rewarding his troops with the plunder of their goods, expelled from the city the remnant of the unbelieving nation." In such contexts, the metaphorical language of cliché seen in phrases like "the sword of persecution" and "episcopal warfare" becomes horridly and shockingly reanimated. The real conflicts make the metaphors of conflict more vivid.

The religious chapters show a marked proliferation of all kinds of metaphor; and the metaphor is used, not to clarify the arguments of the controversialists, but to convey the feelings of the historian. One of Gibbon's longest series of figurative expressions occurs in Chapter XLVII, and it conveys his exasperation at the violence of the verbal disputes about the meaning to be attached to a particular theological doctrine—the doctrine of the unity of the two natures of Christ. Within one short paragraph, the parties to the dispute ransack art and nature for every possible comparison; enlarge an atom to a monster in the polemic microscope; wander through the dark and devious thickets of a theological labyrinth until they meet at either extreme the horrid phantoms of Cerinthus and Apollinaris (who, in this context, seem to have become types of theological Cerberus); recoil from the twilight of sense and heresy; and involve themselves in the gloom of impenetrable orthodoxy, until the breath of prejudice and passion kindles a latent and almost hidden spark (which lingers among the embers of controversy) into a mighty flame of verbal disputes, which shake the pillars of the church and state. Such, in a paraphrase, is the chain of metaphor which tumbles from the historian's pen.

It is difficult to believe that Gibbon's imagination ever functioned in this extraordinarily romantic way until we remember that his mixture and muddle of metaphor is intended to expose the intemperance and insanity of the early church. The church is successively pictured as a victorious army, a zoologist, a traveler in the land of Classical mythology, a lover of obscurity, and, most splendid of all, as a wind which kindles a flame which destroys buildings by shaking them down like Samson! There is more metaphor in this one single paragraph than there is in many another entire chapter of the *History*.

When the verbal battles give place to bloody ones, the exuberance of metaphor is a little chastened; but we may still find wild beasts in the spiritual amphitheater; a flame of heresy extinguished; the rust of antiquity varnishing (an unusual mixture of terminology) a particular doctrine; controversy fermenting; theological insects stinging and distilling their venom in idle fury; seeds both of discord and of faith; and—most memorable of a collocation of fine conceits—Gibbon's description of the formula which defines a disputed doctrine successfully as "the road to paradise, a bridge as sharp as a razor . . . suspended over the abyss by the master-hand of the theological artist." It is easy to see that the abyss is the pit of damnation and that we are saved from it by the skill of a structural engineer, but why should Gibbon have likened the bridge to a razor? Can he have wished us to contrast the theologian's follies with the eminent reasonableness of the philosophical principle known as Ockham's razor and to contrast the product of passion with the method of reason? Certainly anyone who meddled with the doctrine would risk serious (spiritual) injury.

One kind of metaphorical usage which recurs frequently is typical of its century. After giving an account of the sufferings of one of his Christian victims, the historian allows that "Humanity may drop a tear on the fate of Nestorius." The graceful inclination of Humanity (personified, and therefore able to supply the tear) over the grave (turned by the fashion of the time not into death itself but into an abstract fate) is in the style of the weeping nymphs and animated busts which decorate many a storied urn and votive tablet erected above the tombs of the worthy and wealthy dead. Gibbon urges our participation in a formal act of commemoration after the manner of his century—a manner which may be studied in poetic elegies as well as in chiseled marble, a manner which is, in either material, expressive of a feeling real, deep, and sincere, but carefully disciplined.

Personification and abstraction are necessary tools for the expression as well as for the control of emotion, and the implicit metaphor often conveys the historian's feeling. When he writes of "The weight which they [the sectaries] cast into the downfall of the Eastern empire," it is left to the reader to picture the scales which a blind Justice (looking now, perhaps, like a scornful Nemesis) holds out to the warring adversaries; and, if he does so, he will also make the appropriate reflections upon their shortsighted stupidity and fanatical bias. Another implicit metaphor is contained in Gibbon's expectations that "the reader may be amused with the various prospect of" Eastern sects. We are invited to share the detachment of the distant and elevated observer as he gazes upon an extensive view of the religious landscape: if it is not quite from China to Peru, it is at least from Persia to Egypt and Abyssinia.

Such metaphors as these are still referable to things. Very frequently the referents vanish and need some effort of the intellect to be retrieved. What are we expected to visualize when we read that "the only hope of delaying the ruin of the Roman name" depended upon reciprocal help? Is the name a building, a heroine, a business enterprise, or is it, perhaps, the foundation of Roman greatness? When we are told of Pulcheria that "The piety of a Christian virgin was adorned by the zeal and liberality of an empress," we must, perforce, make the effort to view piety as another young lady dressed in the garments of purity and decorated with the jewels, zeal and liberality, or the metaphor goes dead. If we visualize, it is faintly ridiculous: can we perhaps see piety as one of the empress's good angels?

Gibbon's metaphors are not always from his own century. If "the little world of man is perpetually shaken by vice and misfortune," he surely has in mind King Lear, striving "in his little world of man to out-scorn / The to-and-fro-conflicting wind and rain." When "the baseless fabric of the union vanished like a dream," he recalls Prospero dissolving "the baseless fabric of this vision." When Claudius becomes emperor as a result of the murder of Gallienus, we are told that "he might applaud the deed" while "he was innocent of the knowledge of it"; and he is thus likened to Lady Macbeth awaiting the murder of Banquo by the agents of her husband, who commands her to "Be innocent of the knowledge, dearest chuck / Till thou applaud the deed."

Milton comes once or twice under direct contribution—from *Paradise Lost* for the description of the comet Electra which we have noted earlier; and for a footnote comparison of Julian's epic march into Illyricum with the progress of Satan from Hell to the newly created world:

> So eagerly the fiend,
> O'er bog, or steep, through strait, rough, dense, or rare,
> With head, hands, wings, or feet, pursues his way,
> And swims, or sinks, or wades, or creeps, or flies.

More properly under the heading of metaphor comes a sentence in the panegyric upon John the Handsome: "The only defect of this accomplished character was the frailty of noble minds—the love of arms and military glory." Gibbon cannot have been reading *Lycidas* as recently as Book Two of *Paradise Lost*, for the lines of which this statement is a reminiscence read:

> Fame is the spur that the clear spirit doth raise,
> (That last infirmity of noble minds)
> To scorn delights and live laborious days. . . .

There are other kinds of literary reference than the metaphorical in the *History*. Thus Dryden supplies the context of at least three comic and satirical references from *Absalom and Achitophel*. The description of Aëtius as successively "a slave, or at least a husbandman, a travelling tinker, a goldsmith, a physician, a schoolmaster, a theologian, and at last the apostle of a new church . . ." is reminiscent of Dryden's method with Zimri, a man similarly listed as "various," "changeable," "always in the wrong," "Chymist, Fidler, Statesman and Buffoon." The note of the "numerous sons whom so many various mothers bore" to Attila is likewise a recollection of the "several mothers [who / bore] To God-like David several sons before." The Alexandrians, fighting "for the dearest of human rights, religion and property" are like the Londoners who "adored their Fathers' God, and Property." Other recollections of and references to Thomas Gray and Thomas Warton, Voltaire and Lafontaine may be found in the text and in the footnotes of the *History*; and they all demonstrate not only Gibbon's familiarity with the literature of his own and of other centuries but also his ability to use it for critical and comparative purposes with admirable discretion and lightness of touch.

Gibbon's famous style supports the main structure of the *History*, and it enforces the judgments upon the Empire which that structure embodies and implies. It works by involving us, for the most part unconsciously, in the historian's feelings and attitudes. The appearance of impartiality and of judicial certainty is well founded in the mass of historical detail and of anecdote because Gibbon rarely, if ever, passes over an incident or a character without implying approval or disapproval. He values thought and action for their correspondence to the standards of an ideal rationality, and we can enjoy the *History* as a work of art for the merit of its consistency. We are attracted to the maintained perfection of attitude by the variety of methods which are used to sustain it. The *History* is, in the highest sense, amusing; but it is far more than a pleasant diversion. It makes possible a unified view of a vast extent of historical material, and it asserts the possibility and necessity of order as a condition of civilized human existence.

In summing up the effect of such careful art applied to such a weight of learning, we may apply to Gibbon the words of an earlier contemporary: "historians . . . may be considered as satirists, and as satirists most severe; since such are most human actions, that to relate, is to expose them."[3] Edward Young's pithy summary foreshadows the tone and the method of the philosophical historians of his century. The attempt to present a perfectly balanced picture must result in an endless series of entertaining and instructive contrasts between men's aspirations and their achievements. By the subtlety of his stylistic methods, Gibbon arrives at this kind of satire. The style has become the most important instrument of appraisal, and the reader can only understand the historian's judgments, and, perhaps, come to share his sympathies, if he maintains a constant alertness to the implications of the style and form of the work. He who enjoys the style perceives how severe is the judgment which man's own actions make upon himself.

CHAPTER 5

Conclusion

A<small>N</small> adverse critic of Gibbon's irreligion, who described him as "a severe student, a man of pleasure and a man of fashion," was also constrained to admit that the historian's letters were "equally honourable to the head and the heart of the writer." Gibbon's friends esteemed him as a man in whom "the best Sense was always guided by the best Judgement," and one lady who had known and respected him confessed that the *Miscellaneous Works* "make me feel affectionate towards Mr. Gibbon as you certainly see the most amiable parts of his character in these accounts and his letters."[1] This study will have succeeded if it has brought out the essential humanity of the historian, both in his private life and in his writings.

The formality of which he has been accused and the amiable vanity which can be deduced from the *Autobiography* may be corrected from the observations of a guest at one of the Neckers' dinner parties in Lausanne, who thought that no one could have had less of the appearance of announcing his fame or of striving to please than Gibbon showed. This Frenchman confided to his diary: "I do not know why, [but] without his having spoken more than any other, his opinion always prevailed; it is perhaps because he never imposed himself and because each one could believe, if he wished, that he himself held the same opinion independently."[2] Gibbon's gentlemanliness embraced courtesy and warmth, and it embodied that personal modesty and that unwillingness to intrude his private concerns upon the time and feelings of others which made him keep his fatal illness to himself until the last.

If he had any vanity, it was for his achievement and not for himself: "I sometimes reflect with pleasure that my writings will survive me" (*Letters*, III, 159). But a passing observation in Chapter XLI betrays the hopes and fears of the historian about the utility of his great work: "The experience of past faults, which may sometimes correct the mature age of an individual, is seldom profitable to the successive generations of mankind." The reflection is pessimistic: we may deduce from it that the study of history and biography may teach something useful to us as individuals, but it has no influence upon man in the mass. Nevertheless, our trained sensitivity to the historian's innuendo and irony, to his suggestion and his satire, will make us more aware of the refinement and civilization which the pursuit of reason can bring within our reach; whilst his substance—his portraits, his characters, and his vivid delineation of great historical movements—will show us the hourly jeopardy into which human actions put our fondest hopes. In his mature age, each reader of the *History* will find in it a profitable study; and Gibbon has the verdict of nearly two centuries of critical approval to support his expectations.

There have been cavillers enough at the work and at the historian: Samuel Coleridge found his style detestable, his work unphilosophical, and his construction artificial; Thomas Carlyle called his style flowery, his sarcasms wicked, and his notes oppressive; Walter Bagehot charged him with neither expressing nor feeling the essence of the Roman people. But the criticisms are outweighed by the number and splendor of the praises of the *History*, and these have come not only from professional writers and historians, but also from general readers who look to history for entertainment as well as information. Pitboy and prime minister alike have praised the *History* for its hold over their imaginations: "Vividly do I remember bringing the first volume home. With youthful glee I read till a late hour. I slept but little that night; the book haunted my dreams. I woke about four on the bright summer Sunday morning, and went into the fields to read until breakfast time."[3] The experience of Thomas Burt is complemented by that of Winston Churchill: "I was immediately dominated both by the story and the style. All through the long glistening middle hours of the Indian day, from when we quitted stables till the evening shadows proclaimed the hour of Polo, I devoured Gibbon. I rode triumphantly through it from end to end and enjoyed it all."[4]

We may begin to read Gibbon in the hope of instruction, but we continue in the expectation of pleasure and delight. Gibbon's sense of irreverent comedy, his ironic highlighting of the effects of human weaknesses, his admiration of goodness, and his love of grandeur, majesty, and nobility—all of these commend him to us, as a historian, as a stylist, as a pattern of eighteenth-century philosophy and as a man.

Notes and References

Chapter One

1. *Autobiography of Edward Gibbon* as originally edited by Lord Sheffield, with an introduction by J. B. Bury (London. 1907–1950). World's Classics Edition, p. 17. All further references are to this edition.

2. *Letters,* III, 634, May 10, 1786, pp. 45–46. *The Letters of Edward Gibbon,* ed. J. E. Norton, in three volumes (London, 1956). Further references appear in the text.

3. The judgments are those of D. M. Low in *Letters,* I, pp. 387–90, q.v.

4. *Letters,* I, No. 16, October 26, 1757, pp. 73–74.

5. D. M. Low, *Gibbon's Journal* (London, 1929) p. 1xiv.

6. *Letters,* I, 20, February 9, 1758, p. 91.

7. The French text is given in *Letters,* I, 27, August 24, 1758, p. 106.

8. See *Letters,* I, Appendix III, 402–407, for a detailed and concise account of these involved affairs.

9. D. M. Low, *Gibbon's Journal,* entry for December 23, 1762. p. 44. Hereinafter cited as *Journal.*

10. The Journal which he kept in French during his second visit to Lausanne notes his social visits and his opinions of his friends, but it gives far more space to digests of his reading. He wrote long critical notes in a "Recueil" or digest of the many learned Latin tomes which he read in preparation for his Italian tour and for his future studies in Roman history. See G. A. Bonnard, ed., *Le Journal de Gibbon à Lausanne 17 Août 1763–19 Avril 1764* (Lausanne, 1945).

11. In an interesting essay Bonnard points out that many entries in Gibbon's Lausanne Journal seem to pre-suppose an intention to write about Roman history long before this moment. See G. A. Bonnard, "L'importance du deuxième séjour de Gibbon à Lausanne dans la formation de l'historien" (Lausanne, 1944).

12. G. A. Bonnard, ed., *Edward Gibbon, Memoirs of my Life* (London, 1966), p. 210, fragment C.

13. *Ibid.,* p. 208, fragment C.

14. William Hayley, *Poems and Plays* (London, 1785), III, 153; Samuel Parr, ed., *Tracts, by Warburton and a Warburtonian* (London, 1789), p. 192.

15. G. O. Trevelyan, *The American Revolution*, IV (London, 1905–16), 470.

16. Henry Best, *Personal and Literary Memorials* (London, 1829), p. 68.

17. The speech was reported in *The Morning Chronicle*, June 14, 1788 (Bonnard, p. 330, n. 27; Norton *Bibliography*, p. 61). A malicious story suggested that Sheridan's adjective had been less complimentary—not luminous, but voluminous.

18. Norton, *Bibliography*, p. 61, n. 5.

19. J. H. Adeane, ed., *The Girlhood of Maria Josepha Holroyd* (London, 1896), p. 77. See also p. 101 of my text.

20. John, Lord Sheffield, ed., *The Miscellaneous Works of Edward Gibbon Esq.* The second edition. 5 vols. (London, 1814), II, 444.

21. *Ibid.*, II, 456.

22. Gibbon's Swiss friends knew that his corpulence was caused by a hydrocele which tapping would reduce, but dared not mention it to him. *Vie de Société dans le Pays de Vaud*, II, 5. A more detailed account of this malady and its treatment is given by Sir Gavin de Beer, *Gibbon and his World* (London, 1968), pp. 118–21, 129–31.

23. *Letters*, III, 797, March 17, 1792, 249. My translation.

24. R. E. Prothero, ed., *Private Letters of Edward Gibbon*, 2 vols. (London, 1896), II, 400.

Chapter Two

1. Because there is such a large number of editions of the *Decline and Fall*, no detailed references are given for citations from the *History*, but it should be clear from the text in which chapter of the work each extract may be found.

2. G. P. Baker, *Twelve Centuries of Rome* (London, 1936), p. 500.

3. *Ibid.*, p. 511.

4. It may be useful to remember that the Arians believed that the Son of God was created by the Father and that there was therefore a time when he had not existed. Consequently, he was held to occupy a subordinate position in the Trinity.

Chapter Three

1. R. B. Peake, *Memoirs of the Colman Family*, including their correspondence with the most distinguished personages of their time. 2 vols. (London, 1841), I, 395–96.

2. Richard Porson, *Letters to Mr. Archdeacon Travis* (London, 1790), pp. xxix–xxx, cited Norton, *Bibliography,* p. 70.

3. J. H. Adeane, ed., *The Girlhood of Maria Josepha Holroyd,* p. 273.

4. Cf. Chapter IX of the *Decline and Fall.* "The gross appetite of love becomes most dangerous when it is elevated, or rather, indeed, disguised by sentimental passion."

5. Malcolm Muggeridge in "The Happy Historian," a review of Georges A. Bonnard's edition of Gibbon's *Memoirs of My Life* in *The Observer Weekend Review,* October 16, 1966. Muggeridge suggests only that the laughs are frequent in Gibbon's account of Oxford.

6. David Hume's arguments are to be found at the beginning of Part I, Conclusion, *An Enquiry Concerning the Principles of Morals* (London, 1751).

7. Was this admiration of the works of Nature increased and enhanced by the lectures of Dr. Hunter upon anatomy, which the author attended in 1777, and which amused him beyond anything else he ever studied?

Chapter Four

1. Yvor Winters, *In Defence of Reason* (New York, 1947), p. 417.

2. G. B. Hill, ed., *Boswell's Life of Johnson,* revised L. F. Powell, (Oxford, 1934), II, 448.

3. Edward Young, "Preface" to his orthodox satires in *Love of Fame, the Universal Passion* (London, 1728), pages unnumbered.

Conclusion

1. The critic was Thomas Dunbar Whitaker in an unsigned review of the 1814 edition of the *Miscellaneous Works* in the *Quarterly Review,* xiii (January, 1815), 384, 385. The other two judgments are those of Maria Josepha Holroyd, daughter of Lord Sheffield, and of Sarah Martha ("Serena") Holroyd, sister of Lord Sheffield, who was a friend of Mrs. Gibbon in Bath. The phrases are taken from J. H. Adeane, ed., *The Girlhood of Maria Josepha Holroyd,* pp. 266, 372.

2. An extract from the unpublished diary of M. Louis-Francois Guigner de Prangins which appears in P. Kohler, *Madame de Stael au Château de Coppet* (Lausanne, 1929; Paris, 1939), p. 21.

3. *Thomas Burt M.P., D.C.L., Pitman and Privy Councillor, An Autobiography* (London, 1924), pp. 122–23. Burt was born in 1837.

4. Winston S. Churchill, *My Early Life* (London, 1930), p. 125.

Selected Bibliography

BIBLIOGRAPHY

NORTON, J. E., *A Bibliography of the Works of Edward Gibbon.* London: Oxford University Press, 1940. Authoritative, indispensable, entertaining. Contains full bibliographical information, useful historical background, and ample quotations from early critics. It should be used to check information given in the next section.

PRIMARY SOURCES

1.   Shorter Works

Essai sur L'Etude de la Littérature. London: Becket and De Hondt, 1761. An English translation was published by the same firm in 1764, and there were several pirated editions in Gibbon's lifetime. Reprinted in the *Miscellaneous Works.*

Mémoires Littéraires de la Grande Bretagne. Vol. I. London: Becket and De Hondt, 1767.

Mémoires Littéraires de la Grande Bretagne. Vol. II. London: Heydinger, 1768. The only article reprinted from these literary journals in the *Miscellaneous Works* is that on Walpole's *Historic Doubts* in the 1814 edition.

Critical Observations on the Sixth Book of the AEneid. London: Elmsley, 1770. Reprinted in the *Miscellaneous Works.*

A Vindication of Some Passages in the Fifteenth and Sixteenth Chapters of the History of the Decline and Fall of the Roman Empire. By the Author. London: Strahan and Cadell, 1779. Reprinted in the *Miscellaneous Works.*

Mémoire Justificatif pour Servir de Réponse à l'Exposé de la Cour de France. London: n.p., 1779. The first issue has no name of printer or place but the second issue gives the printers' names as Harrison and Brooke, sold by Elmsley. It was reprinted in the *Miscellaneous Works.*

The English Essays of Edward Gibbon. Oxford: Clarendon Press, 1972. Edited by Patricia B. Craddock. Includes all Gibbon's writings in English, early or late, except the autobiographical materials and

Decline and Fall. The essays, fragments and notes are arranged chronologically. They include preliminary notes and planned revisions for *Decline and Fall* and for projected later works.

2.   The *History*

It is still possible to read the *History* in the original quarto edition in many libraries; it gives the feel of the work better than any other; but the outstanding scholarly edition is that of J. B. Bury. Textually, the best edition is that edited by Dr. William Smith from the earlier edition by Dean Milman; and I have used this edition for my quotations within the text. There are many handsome editions which it is a pleasure to use. Either of the two modern abridgements may be found useful.

The History of the Decline and Fall of the Roman Empire. By Edward Gibbon, Esq., Volume the First. London: Strahan and Cadell. Quarto. 1776. The remainder of the history was published by the same printer: volumes II and III, 1781; volumes IV–VI, 1788.
The History of the Decline and Fall of the Roman Empire. By Edward Gibbon. With Notes by Dean Milman and M. Guizot. A new edition with additional notes by William Smith, D.C.L. and LL.D. in eight volumes. London: John Murray, 1854-55.

I have used the 1887 reprint. P. 40 of Miss Norton's *Bibliography*, listed above, shows that the Smith-Milman edition corrects some of the errors in the eighteenth-century editions.
The History of the Decline and Fall of the Roman Empire. By Edward Gibbon. Edited in seven volumes with Introduction, Notes, Appendices and Index, by J. B. Bury. London: Methuen, 1896-1900. Revised 1909-14.

This edition is essential to the student of history. Bury's monumental learning has not been superseded, but editions in the World's Classics Library and Everyman's Library are more easily available for the student of literature.

3.   Abridgements
The Decline and Fall of the Roman Empire. An abridgement by D. M. Low. London: Chatto & Windus, 1960. Republished by Penguin Books in association with Chatto & Windus, 1963.

This edition, running to some 900 pages, gives an excellent idea of the range and scope of the *History*.
Gibbon, The Decline and Fall of the Roman Empire and Other Selections from the Writings of Edward Gibbon. Edited and abridged with an Introduction by Hugh Trevor-Roper. Great Histories 1. New York: Twayne, 1963. Also in paperback in the New English Library in

association with the Washington Square Press. London: NEL 1966. (451 pp.)

Although this contains far less of the *History* than Low's abridgement, it includes useful extracts from the *Autobiography* and the *Vindication*, and an excellent, brief Introduction.

4. Miscellaneous Works

Miscellaneous Works of E.G. . . . With memoirs of his life and writing; composed by himself; illustrated from his letters, with occasional notes and narrative by John [Holroyd] Lord Sheffield, first published in two volumes by Cadell and Davies in 1796, but the much expanded five-volume edition (London: John Murray, 1814) with the same title is the more useful and reliable.

5. Autobiography, Letters and Journals

The life of Gibbon to which all biographers owe most is necessarily his own *Autobiography*, the succinct, entertaining, and occasionally moving account of his life and works compiled after his death by his friend Lord Sheffield from the six separate fragmentary attempts of the historian to write a memoir. Some of the many modern editions of Lord Sheffield's version are listed below, together with editions which make use of materials which the first editor omitted. The six versions were edited and printed by John Murray in 1896. A modification of the more formal portrait is contained in the three volumes of *Letters* edited by Miss J. E. Norton who is responsible for the *Bibliography* of Gibbon's works. The Journals provide additional information. Useful editions of all three categories of biographical information are listed below.

The earliest editions and extracts are to be found in the *Miscellaneous Works*, but the scholar will need to consult the following:

a.   Autobiography

The Autobiographies of Edward Gibbon. Printed verbatim from hitherto unpublished MSS. Edited by John Murray. London: John Murray, 1896. The MSS. are the original six drafts from which Lord Sheffield composed the *Autobiography.*

Memoirs of the Life and Writings of Edward Gibbon. Edited by O. F. Emerson. Boston and London: Ginn and Co., 1898. Claims to be "as accurate and complete an account as can be made from the several sketches left by the historian," and has extensive, helpful notes.

The Memoirs of the Life of Edward Gibbon, with various observations and excursions by himself, edited by George Birkbeck Hill. London: Methuen, 1900. A collation of the 1796 and 1814 editions of the memoir given by Lord Sheffield in the *Miscellaneous Works*. The ample notes are detailed and useful: some Victorian prejudices are amusing.

The Autobiography of Edward Gibbon. As originally edited by Lord Sheffield, with an introduction by J. B. Bury. London: Oxford University Press, 1907. World's Classics Series. Often reprinted.

The Autobiography of Edward Gibbon. Edited with an introduction by Oliphant Smeaton. London: Dent and Dutton, 1911. Everyman Series. Often reprinted.

Edward Gibbon Memoirs of My Life. Edited from the manuscripts by Georges A. Bonnard. London: Nelson, 1966. A new arrangement of the materials contained in the six original versions to give a less formal and more vivid biography than Lord Sheffield's arrangement. Exhaustive notes.

The Autobiography of Edward Gibbon. Edited by Dero A. Saunders. New York: Meridian Books, 1961. A readable edition which considers some of the textual problems.

Gibbon's Autobiography. Edited with an introduction by M. M. Reese. London: Routledge and Kegan Paul, 1971. Attempts to give a more faithful picture of Gibbon's mind and character than Sheffield did, by making some changes. Useful notes for the new student.

b.   Letters

Many letters *to* Gibbon as well as *by* him are contained in the *Miscellaneous Works* and in:

Private Letters of Edward Gibbon (1753-1794). Edited by R. E. Prothero. London: J. Murray, 1896.

The Letters of Edward Gibbon. Edited by J. E. Norton in three volumes. London: Cassell and Co., 1956. This definitive edition may be read for pleasure. The very useful appendices include one by D. M. Low on Gibbon's Latin Letters, and one upon the chronology of his correspondence with Suzanne Curchod.

c.   Journals

Journal de Mon Voyage dans quelques endroits de la Suisse, 1755, in *Miscellanea Gibboniana*. Edited G. R. de Beer and G. A. Bonnard. Lausanne: Publications de la Faculté des Lettres, 1952.

Gibbon's Journal to January 28th, 1763. Introductory Essay by D. M. Low. London: Chatto and Windus, 1929.

Le Journal de Gibbon à Lausanne 17 Août 1763-19 Avril 1764. Publié par Georges Bonnard. Lausanne: F. Rouge & Cie, S.A., 1945.

Gibbon's Journey from Geneva to Rome. His Journal from 20th April to 2nd October, 1764. Edited by Georges A. Bonnard. London: Thomas Nelson and Sons Ltd., 1961. This Journal is in French. The volume includes extracts from the diary of Gibbon's traveling companion, William Guise.

SECONDARY SOURCES

1. Biographies
ADEANE, J. H., ed. *The Girlhood of Maria Josepha Holroyd.* London: Longmans, Green & Co., 1896. Biography of the daughter of Lord Sheffield; contains several references to the historian.
DE BEER, (SIR) GAVIN. *Gibbon and His World.* With 129 black and white plates. London: Thames and Hudson, 1968. Particularly handsome, splendidly illustrated monograph.
FUGLUM, PER. *Edward Gibbon, His View of Life and Conception of History.* Oslo and Oxford: Blackwell, 1953. In the series Oslo Studies in English, Publications of the British Institute, University of Oslo. Concerned more with the historian's opinions than with his life.
JOYCE, MICHAEL. *Edward Gibbon.* London: Longmans, Green, 1953. Men and Books Series. Lively, informative biography with some pleasing criticism of the *History.*
LOW, D. M. *Edward Gibbon, 1737-1794.* London: Chatto and Windus, 1937. Scholarly and attractive biography by the editor of the Journal; enjoyable, admirable, sensitive, and complete.
MORISON, JAMES COTTER. *Gibbon.* London: Macmillan, 1878. Often reprinted; in English Men of Letters Series. Useful, distinctively nineteenth-century view of the man and the work.
ROBERTSON, J. M. *Gibbon.* London: Watts & Co., 1925. Life Stories of Famous Men. Rationalist apologia for a rationalist historian.
SÉVERY, M. et Mme. W. de. *La Vie de Société dans le Pays de Vaud.* Lausanne & Paris: Bridel & Fischbacher, 1911, 1912. Vol. I. includes biographies of Gibbon's friends Salomon and Catherine de Sévery. Vol II. contains chapters on Gibbon and Wilhelm de Sévery.
SWAIN, JOSEPH WARD. *Edward Gibbon the Historian.* New York: St. Martin's Press, 1966. London: Macmillan, 1966. Almost entirely biographical account of the shaping of the *History.*

YOUNG, GEORGE M. *Gibbon.* London: Peter Davies, 1932. New editions: London: Nelson, 1939, and Rupert Hart-Davies, 1948. Succinct and elegant account of the historian, full of fruitful suggestions for study.

2.   Critical Studies

BAGEHOT, WALTER. *The Collected Works of Walter Bagehot.* Edited by Norman St. John-Stevas. 8 Vols. London: The Economist, 1965. Vol. I contains an entertaining brief biography full of engaging prejudices.

BLACK, J. B. *The Art of History. Study of Four Great Historians of the Eighteenth Century.* London: Methuen, 1926. The other three historians are Voltaire, Hume, and Robertson.

BOND, HAROLD L. *The Literary Art of Edward Gibbon.* Oxford: Clarendon Press, 1960. Outstanding analysis of the art of Gibbon's prose; does not quite do justice to his construction of the *History*.

BRAUDY, LEO B. *Narrative Form in History and Fiction.* Princeton, N.J.: Princeton University Press, 1970. Studies the implications of Gibbon's narrative stance in the last section of the book, comparing his art with that of the eighteenth-century novelist.

BUTTERFIELD, HERBERT. *Christianity in European History.* London: Oxford University Press, 1951. Contains helpful comments on the reign of Julian.

COLERIDGE, S. T. "Table Talk." August 15, 1833. In *Coleridge's Miscellaneous Criticism.* Edited by T. M. Raysor. London: Constable, 1936. Romantic reaction to rationality.

DAWSON, CHRISTOPHER. *Edward Gibbon. Proceedings of the British Academy*, XX (London: Humphrey Milford, 1934), 160 *et. seq.* Published as separate pamphlet. Shows how Gibbon united the humanist tradition with the philosophic culture of the eighteenth century and the historiography of the Roman Church.

ELTON, OLIVER. "Gibbon." *A Survey of English Literature 1730-1780.* 2 Vols. London: Arnold, 1928. II, 283-300. Succinct account and appraisal of the life and work.

FUSSELL, PAUL. *The Rhetorical World of Augustan Humanism, Ethics and Imagery from Swift to Burke.* London: Oxford University Press, 1965. Useful comments on Gibbon's imagery and ideas.

JORDAN, DAVID P. *Gibbon and his Roman Empire.* Urbana, Chicago, London: University of Illinois Press, 1971. Series of studies showing influence of Gibbon's life, of his sources and of his other reading upon the composition of the *History*.

McCLOY, SHELBY T. *Gibbon's Antagonism to Christianity*. Chapel Hill: University of North Carolina Press, 1933. Describes Gibbon as "an agnostic, a fighter for tolerance, and a respecter of sincere and unostentatious religion." Details the attacks on Gibbon's irreligion.

SAINTE-BEUVE. C. A. "Gibbon." *Causeries de Lundi*. VIII. (August 29, 1853). 430-72. Paris: Garnier Frères, 3rd edition. Biographical account which maintains that Gibbon is, in some respects, a French writer.

WHITE, LYNN T. Jr., ed. *The Transformation of the Roman World, Gibbon's Problem after Two Centuries*. Berkeley and Los Angeles: University of California Press, 1966. London: Cambridge University Press, 1966. Key criticism of Gibbon as a historian which includes the extreme view that "as history, his work is almost unbelievably obsolete, save for antiquarian details."

WINTERS, YVOR. "The Writing of History." *In Defense of Reason*. New York: Swallow Press and William Morrow and Co., 1947. Perceptive remarks on historians of the Enlightenment.

3.   Historical Bibliography

Students of history will go to modern works to modify Gibbon's pictures of the Eastern and Western Empires and of Europe in the Dark Ages. The *Cambridge Ancient History*, ed. J. B. Bury and others, University Press, Cambridge 1923 onwards, and in particular the 1970 revision of Volume I. *The Cambridge Mediaeval History*. Planned by J. B. Bury, eds. various, University Press, Cambridge 1911 onwards, and in particular the rewritten Volume IV, *The Byzantine Empire*, ed. J. M. Hussey, two parts, University Press, Cambridge, 1966, 1967 should be consulted. In addition the following works may be found useful.

BAKER, G. P. *Twelve Centuries of Rome*. London: Bell and Sons, 1936. Popular history of the Empire. I have cited his descriptions of Julian and Constantine.

BAYNES, N. H. *The Byzantine Empire*. London: Williams & Norgate, 1925. Home University Library. Brief history by an expert in the field.

BAYNES, N. H., & MOSS, H. St. L. B., eds. *Byzantium*. Oxford: Clarendon Press, 1948 and 1953. A collection of essays on aspects of Byzantine culture, administration, and economics by recognized authorities; brief but comprehensive.

BURY, J. B. *The Invasion of Europe by the Barbarians*. London: Macmillan and Co., 1928. Learned work by the great editor of Gibbon.

DAWSON, CHRISTOPHER. *The Making of Europe. An introduction to the History of European Unity*. London: Sheed & Ward, 1932. Reprinted without bibliography. Cleveland and New York: The World Publishing Co., 1956 and subsequently. Meridian Books M 35. Traces the growth of Catholic Europe from the institutions of the Roman Empire.

DOPSCH, ALFONS. *The Economic and Social Foundations of European Civilization*. London: Kegan Paul & Co., 1937. Condensed by Erna Patzelt from the second German edition of *Wirtschaftliche und Soziale Grundlagen der Europäischen Kulturentwicklung aus der Zeit von Caesar bis auf Karl den Grossen*, and translated by M. G. Beard and Nadine Marshall. Shows that neither the Germans nor any one else destroyed any essential part of the Roman heritage.

HUSSEY, J. M. *The Byzantine World*. London: Hutchinson's University Library, 1957 and 1961. One of the best brief outlines of Byzantine history and culture.

MATTINGLY, H. *Roman Imperial Civilization*. London: Arnold, 1957. New York: St. Martin's Press, 1957. Luminous, detailed account of Roman institutions and culture.

OSTROGORSKY, G. *History of the Byzantine State*. Oxford: Basil Blackwell, 1956. Perhaps the outstanding scholarly study of the Byzantine state and an acknowledged classic. Contains a critical study of the work of his predecessors.

PIRENNE, H. *Mohammed and Charlemagne*. London: G. Allen and Unwin, 1939. Translated from French by B. Miall. Shows a decisive change in the eighth century, when the Muslims blocked the West Mediterranean, producing a new northern focus in Europe, represented by the Carolingian Empire.

ROSTOVTSEFF, M. I. *The Social and Economic History of the Roman Empire*. Second edition revised by P. M. Fraser. Oxford: Clarendon Press, 1957. 2 vols. Truly monumental description of Roman life and economic conditions throughout the Empire. Detailed treatment of the second and third centuries.

RUNCIMAN, SIR STEVEN. *Byzantine Civilisation.* London: Arnold, 1933. Reprinted London: Methuen, University Paperbacks, 1961. Describes institutions and aspects of life in the Byzantine world with a wealth of pithy illustration.

———. *A History of the Crusades.* London: Cambridge University Press, 1951-54. 3 vols. Complete antidote to Gibbon's views.

THOMPSON, E. A. *A History of Attila and the Huns.* Oxford: Clarendon, 1948. Scholarly study showing that Attila was neither a military genius nor an outstanding diplomat, but a leader who foresaw the uses to which the power of a united Hun society could be put, and demonstrating that the Huns were mere plunderers and marauders.

VASILIEV, A. A. *History of the Byzantine Empire.* Madison, Wis., 1928, and Oxford: Basil Blackwell, 1952. Revised one-vol. edition. Russian view of the Empire, first published 1917; meticulous, scholarly, and authoritative. Cites in translation many opinions of Russian historians. Clear, reliable guide to the study of Byzantine history.

VOGT, JOSEPH. *The Decline of Rome. The Metamorphosis of Ancient Civilisation.* Translated from the German by Janet Sondheimer. London: Weidenfeld and Nicholson, 1967. History of Mediterranean civilization, and particularly of the West, during the last centuries of the Ancient World (A.D. 200-500) revealing the roots of modern Western culture.

WALBANK, F. W. *The Awful Revolution. The Decline of the Roman Empire in the West.* Toronto: University of Toronto Press, 1968. Brief summary of the causes of collapse, related to conditions in the modern world. Attributes decline to undeveloped technology and failure of organization.

WALLACE-HADRILL, J. M. *Early Germanic Kingship in England and on the Continent.* Oxford: Clarendon Press, 1971. Discusses Germanic political and social concepts of kingship, law etc., with reference to the Roman Empire.

4. General Interest

TUCKER, SUSIE I. *Enthusiasm A study in semantic change.* Cambridge: Cambridge University Press, 1972. Entertaining and erudite commentary upon eighteenth-century attitudes to enthusiasm with copious illustration.

Index